ENJOYING THE ARTS/MUSIC

ENJOYING THE ARTS

Music

By

David S. Rattner

Illustrated by

Nancy Lou Gahan

RICHARDS ROSEN PRESS, INC.
New York, N.Y. 10010

for
Henriette, Nina, Bill
and Matthew

Published in 1976 by Richards Rosen Press, Inc.
29 East 21st Street, New York, N.Y. 10010

First Edition

Manufactured in the United States of America

Library of Congress Cataloging in Publication Data

Rattner, David.
  Enjoying the arts.

  (Enjoying the arts series)
  Includes indexes.
  SUMMARY: A guide to the appreciation of serious
music which discusses the elements of music; the
instruments of the orchestra; forms such as opera,
ballet, program music, and chamber music; and composers and their contributions.
  1. Music—Analysis, appreciation. [1. Music—
Analysis, appreciation]   I. Title.

MT6.R245E5   780′.15   75–19258

ISBN 0–8239–0332–X

ABOUT THE AUTHOR

DAVID RATTNER was born in New York City and educated at the Juilliard School of Music and Columbia University. He also studied at New York University. While still a student, he played piano and double-bass professionally, but soon established a career as a music teacher in New York City high schools. Appointed to the High School of Music and Art, he helped develop many  new courses in that school's early years, teaching the first classes in composition, conducting and music history. He then became Chairman of Music at Fort Hamilton High School, and later held the same post at James Madison High School and finally at Abraham Lincoln High School. For many years he conducted the All-City High School Orchestra, a specially selected group of the most talented instrumentalists in all the high schools of the city. He also conducted the New York City Teachers' Orchestra.

Always eager to secure a more important role for music in the curriculum, Mr. Rattner served as Chairman of the Standing Committee for Music for the Board of Education and as President of the Music Chairmen's Association of New York City. He has been active in the training and selection of teachers and has given in-service courses for them.

He is deeply interested in the theatre and has done extensive work in dramatics, both in schools and in summer camps. A Ford

v

Foundation Fellowship whetted an appetite for travel, and he has visited many of the world's cultural centers.

Now retired, after thirty-seven years of teaching, Mr. Rattner continues working with retired adults.

CONTENTS

I

PARTICIPANT LISTENING

THE ART OF LISTENING TO SERIOUS MUSIC

If you have ever attended an outdoor symphony concert at Tanglewood, Robin Hood Dell, Ravinia Park, the Hollywood Bowl, or the many other spots in the United States where outdoor summer concerts are popular, you might have noticed that people listen to serious music in many different ways and on many different levels. At Tanglewood, for instance, as one walks from the gate toward the great open shed that shelters the orchestra and the holders of the more expensive tickets, one notices that some people have spread blankets on the grass rather far from the shed. Here the music, dimmed somewhat by the distance from the orchestra, will provide a pleasant background for a picnic, a quiet conversation or, in the shaded areas, more romantic pursuits. Closer to the shed where the music can be clearly heard but the orchestra is not seen, one finds those who have come just to listen, some lying back on blankets while they watch the clouds (or in the evening, the stars) and daydream or think or concentrate. Others are sitting with the musical score in their laps, intent on following every note as their special musical training has taught them. Inside the shed, the audience, seated in concert hall style, is much like the audience at any indoor concert—confirmed music lovers, generally older (and more affluent) than the outdoor group—who have come to listen to great music played by a great orchestra and to watch a great conductor in much the same way that they attend concerts all winter long.

Many people enjoy having music as a background for work or study, and research has indicated that when music is piped into a factory assembly line area, worker output increases. Students fre-

1

quently claim they concentrate better and accomplish more when the hi-fi or the radio is going while they work. Just why this is so has never been fully explained, but one theory holds that monotonous work or work done in isolation is "lonely" and produces "anxieties," and music takes the edge off this "loneliness," thus freeing the worker or student for better effort.

Another factor is the socializing force exerted by music. The restaurant that pipes in recorded music creates an atmosphere and attracts a clientele that reflects musical as well as culinary preferences. Quiet dinner music is likely to accompany an elaborate menu, while the hamburger joint will feature the juke box and rock and roll. The carousel, the carnival, the circus raise spirits high for crowds of people with exciting, lively music. The band at the head of a parade of soldiers inspires courage and patriotism (as did the war dance of tribal days), and ceremonies and rituals such as inaugurations, coronations, graduations, weddings, funerals and worship are celebrated and solemnized with the unifying effect of music. For nothing speaks so directly and so universally to our emotions, be they wild, exalted, humorous, solemn or tragic, as does music.

Some, however, enjoy musical stimulation of the emotions and the imagination on a more individual basis and will prefer just listening at home alone. Here, in complete privacy, one can feel heroic, tender, passionate, playful, tearful, mean, mysterious or peaceful without revealing any of these hidden depths in public. Or one can assume a mask of sophistication (a poker face) and enjoy the same wide range of feeling at a live concert, displaying nothing of his secret self.

Just as music ignites the emotions, it fires the imagination. It can summon up stories, real or imagined, of kings and heroes, of blissful or doomed loves, of noble or sinful lives. It can conjure up visions of heaven or hell, of peace or war, of city or country, of land or sea, of sunshine or storm, of confidence or doubt. These visions, however, originate with the listener, for the composer may not have had any intention of communicating the specific image, story or feeling with which that particular listener responds. Often a number of listeners will describe totally different reactions to the same piece of music.

And sometimes the composer, by use of a suggestive title or an explanatory note, will chart the imaginative course for the listener. Titles like *Lament* or *Footprints in the Snow* are self-explanatory and dictate certain responses.

Most of us also react physically to music. This is hardly surprising since the human body is a rhythmic organism. Our hearts beat rhythmically, and we breathe and walk and run rhythmically. Our voices rise in pitch when we are excited and fall when we are depressed. We make instantaneous connection between what we hear and body movements. A noise will cause us to stop in our tracks, turn our head, raise an arm protectively or run. When we hear an insistent rhythm we pick it up and drum a finger to it or tap a foot. When long continued, the effect can become hypnotic and soon the whole body responds. But rhythm is only one musical element. We respond to loudness and softness, physically straining to hear the latter, and alternatingly retreating from or exultantly rising to meet the onslaught of the former. We thrill to the challenging tones of the brass instruments; we bathe in the sensuous sighing of the strings; we fly with the high woodwinds and hobble along with the bassoons and do battle with the percussion. We literally surround ourselves with stereophonic sound and glory in the fullness of it.

We can listen in any or all of these ways, and most of us do try them all without being aware of it. But the most satisfying listening is the kind in which the listener participates with greatest awareness. He who listens and feels and dreams and wallows in the sheer sound is enjoying a much richer experience than someone who studies or works with music in the background. And that experience can be made richer still by bringing to it information about the composer, about the period in which it was written and about the music itself. The information need not be technical, but it is amazing how much the inexperienced ear can be trained to listen for.

Since we are here exploring the art of "participant listening," we will concern ourselves mainly with those factors that help develop listening skills. How can we hear more and better? How can we focus on important points in the music without losing them in the general sound? For while it is fine to have a rich background in music

3

history or a full training in the specialized aspects of composition and performance, it is, nevertheless, possible to enjoy serious music on a level of deep appreciation with only a smattering of relatively non-technical guidance. Then, as interest increases, and good music has an uncanny way of generating ever increasing interest, the participant listener can take steps to broaden his background through more reading and more listening experience.

II

THE STUFF OF MUSIC

MELODY, RHYTHM, HARMONY, DYNAMICS, TONE COLOR

Melody

We can begin to improve our listening abilities by pinpointing the important elements of music. Two of these, melody and rhythm, are so fundamental that the untrained listener tends not to think of them separately. When we hum a melody we hum not only its notes but its rhythms. We learned them in their togetherness and for most of us that's the only way we can recognize them. And yet they exist separately and are treated separately by composers.

Melody is simply a succession of notes sounded one after another. We sometimes refer to a "melodic line" since any succession of notes seems to string out in a line. Melody probably began when primitive man found his voice. It can be heard in the howls of animals (recently a recording was made of wolf calls which were classified by melodic differences), in the song of birds, in the roaring winds and in many twentieth century noises such as fire sirens, the hum of machines, etc. It changes character for different ethnic groups. We westerners tend to limit our melodies to the notes of the diatonic scale (do, re, mi, fa, sol, la, ti, do) but elsewhere on this earth people use many more notes or sometimes fewer notes. We tend to move from note to note directly, but people in the Near East tend to slide from note to note in a wailing fashion.

For the greater part of the music that figures in standard concert programs today (music of the seventeenth, eighteenth, nineteenth, and much of the twentieth centuries) melody is very carefully or-

5

ganized and very skillfully manipulated by the composer. He may repeat a short melodic idea (motive) or he may use the idea as a pattern and repeat it at different pitch levels, that is to say, in sequence. Or he may turn it upside down or backwards. He can write a rising melody which generally builds tension and excitement or a descending melody which generally lessens tension. He can write in either mode of the diatonic scale, the major or the more plaintive minor mode, or in modes characteristic of the early church or of special ethnic groups. So it behoves the listener to become aware of and to recognize the melodies used in whatever music he is exposed to. If you can recognize the tune each time it returns you're a long way toward understanding the music. If you can hum the tune then you've really sunk your teeth into the problem.

Rhythm

With rhythm, definitions become harder because there are many related and overlapping terms that confuse things. Rhythm, tempo, meter, time, beat, measure and many others must really be explored before one gets the whole picture.

Melody concerns itself with a succession of notes or pitches (high or low). Rhythm concerns itself with how long each note or pitch should last. And all those other terms are basically concerned, in one way or another, with the same thing, the duration of the sound. Just as Western music builds most of its melodies around the scale, so it tends to organize its rhythms into certain familiar patterns. Much of our music falls into a two, three or four beat pattern with stressed notes or pulsations coming every second, third or fourth beat. However, our response to rhythm is generally more immediate and complete than our response to melody and we can pick up and recognize very intricate and varied rhythms very quickly. So it is not surprising that we adopt the rhythms of other lands and peoples more readily than we accept their melodic idioms. Western music has made great use of African, Indian, Polynesian, Caribbean rhythms, and American jazz with its endlessly varied and inventive rhythms has influenced music all over the world.

6

Rhythm can exert its appeal quite separately from the other musical elements. We can listen to a drummer, follow the changing patterns he produces, or be almost hypnotized by insistent repetition. For most of us, however, melody coexists with its built in rhythms. Even so, the balance between rhythm and melody is constantly changing. A march melody has within it the feeling of a march, and it is its rhythm that gives the melody its special character. The same is true for most dance tunes, but in a love song or a lullaby the interest lies more in the melodic line than in the underlying rhythm.

Before leaving rhythm, we should clarify some terminology. Most authorities define rhythm as the pattern of duration note by note (how long each note lasts). Meter or beat is defined as the regular interval of accent—every two, every three or every four beats—and is sometimes related to the rhythms of poetry (dactylic, iambic, trochaic, etc). Tempo has to do with the over all pace and mood of the music, fast or slow or in between, and tempo markings are usually in Italian (*adagio*—slow, *vivace*—lively, *presto*—fast). Generally speaking, fast rhythms, like rising melodies, tend to build tension and excitement and slow ones to lessen tension. But rhythms, fast or slow, can be made interesting and exciting by placing accents in unexpected places (syncopation) or by introducing other irregularities.

Both melody and rhythm are the result of the composer's genius and creativity and are infinitely varied. For easy understanding we mentioned melodies based on the diatonic scale and only two, three or four beat rhythms. But melodies and rhythms are not limited by these patterns. The eager listener must learn to recognize and remember tunes in whatever balance of melody and rhythm and however innovative and original they are. For memory will be the key to further understanding.

Harmony

If melody is defined as the sounding of notes one after the other, then harmony is defined as the sounding of two or more notes at the same time. The development of harmony comprises a long and com-

7

plicated history, but for our purposes, we must be aware that harmony is achieved in either of two basic ways. The first is by combining independent melodies in such a way that they fit in with each other. A simple illustration can be made by having one person sing *Three Blind Mice* while another sings *Frère Jacques* at the same time. The effect is pleasing and produces "harmony." When harmony is the result of combining melodic lines we call it *counterpoint*. Counterpoint (or contrapuntal music) figured very prominently in the music of the seventeenth and early eighteenth centuries and is still and has always been a very important compositional technique. Counterpoint is often referred to as polyphony (many parts or melodies).

The other way in which harmony is achieved is by fitting a melody with an accompaniment of appropriate but purely supportive or background sounds called chords. Here, of course, the single melody holds the chief interest since it doesn't have to share the spotlight with another melody. Such music is called homophonic (one accompanied melody) as opposed to polyphonic. Chords are what the guitarist strums when he accompanies a singer. However chords are interesting in their own right. Some chords are restful and static, but some create a tension that demands the music move on to another chord. These, the musician says, require resolution. The story is told that when Handel, the composer of *Messiah*, was a small boy and had been sent upstairs to bed, he was listening to music being played downstairs. The music broke off unexpectedly on the chord before the very last and Handel could not sleep until he had run downstairs and played the final chord. Whether the story is true or not, it demonstrates the power of certain chords to move the music along. Other chords create atmosphere and are ominous, mysterious, harsh, bright, etc. While all chords are harmonic they are not necessarily harmonious or pleasing. Harmony makes frequent use of discordant sound, sometimes to heighten the pleasure of the resolution to a concordant or pleasing sound which follows the discord, but also because sometimes discord is appropriate to the purposes of the composer.

Harmony has developed in such sophisticated ways that frequently

8

it competes with melody and rhythm for listener interest. In other words, some music attracts through the richness of its harmonic texture rather than with its striking melodies or interesting rhythms. It is possible to learn to recognize certain harmonic styles and idioms just as one learns to recognize melodies and rhythms. Humming them, however, may prove more difficult!

No discussion of melody and harmony is complete without some consideration of key. This is the feeling that much music engenders of wanting to end on the note on which it began, or at least on the same chord. It was very important in the seventeenth and eighteenth centuries, but as composers in the nineteenth century became more adventurous harmonically, they changed "key" very frequently (modulated) and the importance of returning to the "home key" gradually lessened, until today much music is written atonally (in no particular key) or polytonally (in several keys at one time).

Dynamics

Dynamic means forceful and comes from the Greek word for power. Musicians use the word dynamics to refer to the whole world of effects made possible when varying degrees of force or power are used in producing a sound. Everyone reacts to loudness or softness and skillful composers make the most of these reactions. Schubert, for instance, opens the *Unfinished Symphony* with a very soft melody played by the low strings (cellos and basses). The effect is mysterious and suspenseful. Later the same melody returns played by the entire orchestra, strings, winds and brass full blast, and the effect is aggressive and assertive and monumentally strong. Each version creates interest and tension, but of totally different kinds. The famous opening four notes of Beethoven's *Fifth Symphony* are among the most forceful and challenging utterances in music. They have been likened by critics and historians to Beethoven's hurling his fist in defiance and anger at the fate which had made him deaf. Again they are played full force by the whole orchestra and repeated immediately, a tone lower in sequence, with equal strength. After a dramatic silence, the original four notes are repeated, this time softly with only violins playing somewhat more rapidly, and the effect is one of nervous agitation, totally different from the first version, although the notes are exactly the same. Contrast between loud and soft lends interest and drama to music, but so does the gradual build-up of volume from the very soft to the very loud, an effect we call *crescendo*. *Crescendo* can be achieved by a soloist simply by singing or playing with gradually added force and this is also true of groups such as choruses or orchestras. But an even more dramatic *crescendo* can be achieved by groups by starting softly with only a few performers and then adding players or singers a few at a time until finally a point is reached where everyone is doing his utmost. This is called a cumulative *crescendo*. Rossini, the composer of the operas *William Tell* and *The Barber of Seville* is known for such *crescendos* built up from a mere whisper to raging thunder over a fairly long stretch of orchestral music.

The reverse, the *diminuendo* or *decrescendo*, usually achieves a lessening of tension, an easing off of the dramatic in the music as it gets softer and less forceful. But Tchaikovsky, in the final bars of the *Pathétique* Symphony carries a *diminuendo* to the extreme of virtual inaudibility, creating a feeling of inexpressible sadness and unbearable grief.

Dynamic markings in music are mostly based on the two Italian words *piano* (soft) and *forte* (strong or loud). The most frequently used markings are listed here:

> p = *piano* = soft
> pp = *pianissimo* = very soft
> mp = *mezzo piano* = medium soft (louder than p)
> f = *forte* = loud
> ff = *fortissimo* = very loud
> mf = *mezzo forte* = medium loud (less loud than f)

In the Tchaikovsky passage mentioned above the composer marks the last bars *pppp* and elsewhere in the same symphony he calls for a passage at *ffff*. For the tail end of the nineteenth century when the *Pathétique* was composed this probably marked the loudest possible sound the orchestra could produce. Today with electronic amplification so much a part of the instrumental scene there seems to be no limit to loudness.

We have so far dealt with dynamics in the broad outlines of a piece, but of course many small and detailed effects are possible. For instance, a single note may be attacked strongly and then softened immediately after the strong attack without breaking the continuity of sound so that for the remainder of its duration it is a soft note. The effect is called *forte-piano* and its sign is *fp*. A *crescendo* can occur on a single long note as can a *decrescendo*. In music for groups one part of the group may be performing a *crescendo* while another is performing a *decrescendo*. Even the two hands of the pianist may be working at different dynamic levels and frequently the pianist is asked to create different levels with different fingers of the same hand. Sometimes a long build up of tone is interrupted with a *subito piano* (suddenly soft) so that a climax will not be reached too soon and the *crescendo* can begin again at a lower level.

There is a close interrelationship between rhythm and dynamics, especially when we deal with isolated loud notes (or individually accented notes). Such notes are produced with added force and so are dynamically changed. But since they also produce an accent or pulsation they affect the rhythmic configuration of the music. When a hypnotically repetitive rhythm is dynamically reinforced by ever increasing volume, the effect is overwhelming, as in Ravel's *Bolero*.

Tone Color

When two different instruments play exactly the same pitch we can tell them apart. We know the violin sounds different from the trumpet and both sound different from the piano and all three sound different from you when you sing the same note. Since the pitch for all is the same and since no rhythm or harmony is produced (and we will assume there is no significant difference in dynamic level), the difference is really a separate musical element which we refer to as tone color or tone quality or by the French word *timbre*.

There is, of course, a scientific explanation for what causes these differences in tone colors involving terms like partials and overtones, and it can usually be found in any good physics textbook in the section on sound. But the fact that the differences exist opens up a whole spectrum of tonal possibilities for the composer and his audience to explore and enjoy. So challenging are these possibilities that in the field of popular music they have given rise to a specialist, the arranger, who takes a popular tune and works it over for various combinations of instruments and voices. (Of course he also arranges some of the rhythms and harmonies and even makes melodic changes.) The result is that we can enjoy many widely different versions of the same "pop" number featuring different instrumental and vocal combinations. These arrangers will sometimes take a great melody from some serious masterwork and by adding a "rhythm section" and giving the melody to a saxophone (or, in pop style, to a trumpet or trombone, or clarinet) transform it into a candidate for the "top ten."

But the composer of "serious" music is usually his own arranger and must choose the best vehicle for his musical ideas. Is this music best suited for piano alone, piano and voice, piano and a stringed instrument (violin, viola, cello, bass) or a flute or other woodwind, or a horn or other brass, or a chorus or a string quartet or an orchestra? And even when he has made the determination, what are the tonal possibilities within the confines of his choice (what many different things can the instrument[s] do)?

Just as an example let us briefly consider the violin. Basically, the tone is produced by drawing the bow across the strings. But the bow can bite into the string producing a tone with a good attack, or it can float across the strings producing a smooth light tone. It can bounce on the string, it can connect or disconnect the tones. If used midway between bridge and fingerboard it produces its clearest most open tone, but if moved nearer to the edge of the fingerboard the tone muffles somewhat. If the bow is moved closer to the bridge the tone becomes hollow, etc., etc. The strings can be plucked (*pizzicato*) or struck with the wood of the bow (*col legno*). The finger pressing the string can vibrate (*vibrato*). It can play two or more notes at one time by pressing the bow against two or three strings simultaneously (double-stopping) thus producing a harmonic effect. By placing a weight on the bridge it can be muted (*con sordino*), and the muted violin tone is particularly warm and beautiful. Books have been written on the tonal and technical possibilities of the violin. But a musician trying only the techniques we mentioned changes the instrument's tone color although it remains recognizable as a violin in contrast to other stringed instruments, brasses, woodwinds or the percussion instruments.

What we have discovered about the violin is true of any instrument, even the more mechanical piano, where a system of keys and hammers must be manipulated to make the music. Good pianists can make those keys and hammers respond in different ways and produce different tone colors which they can vary further with the pedals.

Perhaps the most direct control over tone color is reserved for the singer, who, like an actor, can change his voice to imitate other voices or sounds. In Schubert's famous song *The Erlking* the composer and poet (Goethe) describe a father riding through the night with his dying son in his arms in an effort to get help. The son in his delirium sees the Erlking (Death) who tries to claim him. The father tries to calm the boy as the wild ride continues. The singer must describe the ride and sing all three parts, father, son, and Erlking, giving each a distinctive character or tone color. And finally he must convey the tragedy of the boy's death.

When a composer has explored all the tonal possibilities of the individual instruments and voices, he is then faced with the limitless number of possible combinations. And each combination has a distinctive tone color. In his overture *Romeo and Juliet* Tchaikovsky has written an exquisitely beautiful "love theme" which is world famous. It is played by the violas and English horn (an alto oboe) in unison. If one were to hear the violas and English horn play it separately in succession, one would hear the same beautiful melody, in a different tone color in each performance. But both renditions would fall short compared with the warmth, richness and subdued passion of the combined tone qualities the composer wanted.

We have suggested that the listener recognize and memorize

melodies, harmonic styles, rhythm patterns; that he develop a sensitivity to dynamic levels. Now we are suggesting that he learn to recognize instruments and voices. Perhaps this seems like an impossible task. But it only requires a little determination. The ear is a remarkably sensitive organ and the memory very retentive when challenged. And when one concentrates on a piece of music one likes, much can be learned. In other words one can learn from relatively few works how to hang on to melodies and harmonies and rhythms and to be aware of dynamic and instrumental changes. One of the glories of serious music is that it so richly repays repeated listening because one continually discovers and hears new things in it. You will not hear everything at once, and you must not demand too much of yourself at the beginning. But when you really know the melody you will gradually become aware of its rhythms and its harmonies. You will then want to know what instruments play it, and you will begin to appreciate the many musical tricks the composer performs with it.

III

~~~~~~

THE ORCHESTRA

~~~~~~

STRINGS, WOODWINDS, BRASSES, PERCUSSION AND OTHERS

Lest we lose sight of the forest while looking at all the trees, we will turn our attention now to the symphony orchestra, one of the largest and most complex makers of music. We cannot begin to explore its details in a book of this length. And yet it is precisely because of this that we start with the orchestra.

Let us carry the analogy of the forest a step further. Anyone can enjoy the cool shade of the trees, the way the sun creeps through in isolated rays that dapple the leaves, the softness of the ground underfoot and all the overall impressions that forests create. Similarly, we can all experience the fear of getting lost or meeting up with some wild animal. But it is only after we have been in the forest a while that we begin to notice specific trees and to search out the wildlife.

So with the orchestra. We are impressed with its sonorities and its energy, with its constantly changing sound and its wide dynamic range. Its bigness is in itself attractive and interesting. It is only when we get past this bigness that we begin to hear the separate sections and the separate instruments.

The symphony orchestra we meet in the concert hall today is the result of a long chronological development. The seventeenth century orchestra consisted mainly of strings (violins, violas, cellos and basses) with keyboard support (mostly the harpsichord—the piano hadn't been invented yet) and featuring an occasional solo flute, oboe or trumpet. These groups were usually small, seldom numbering more than twenty to twenty-five players. By the second half of

15

the eighteenth century, more players were added including horns, bassoons, and percussion bringing the number up to thirty to thirty-five. With the nineteenth century we hit fifty players with additional percussion, clarinets and trombones. Today we average one hundred players and a fairly set listing of instruments. It should be noted that we are dealing with what is generally regarded as the standard orchestra. But history tells us that in Biblical times and right on through the various intervening cultures, large groups of contemporary instruments were used for special occasions. Some of these instruments were forerunners of present day instruments and some became obsolete. We have no records or manuscripts to give us any indication of what kind of music was played in these early periods since our modern system of notation began its long, slow growth during the Middle Ages.

The modern symphony orchestra consists of four main sections:

I The strings
> violins—usually divided into two sections of 18 first violins and 16 second violins
> violas—numbering 14
> violoncellos—usually shortened to cellos; numbering 12
> contrabasses or double basses or just basses numbering 10

II The woodwinds
> flutes—usually 3 players one of whom doubles on the piccolo—a little flute
> oboes—usually 3 players one of whom doubles on the English horn—or alto oboe
> clarinets—3 players one of whom doubles on the Eb clarinet—a small clarinet and also on the bass clarinet—a large clarinet
> bassoons—3 players one of whom doubles on the contrabassoon—a large bassoon

III Brasses
> French horns—at least 4, more often 6 and sometimes 8 players

trumpets—usually 3 players
trombones—usually 3 players one of whom plays
bass trombone
tuba—one player
IV Percussion
timpani—1 player
snare drum ⎫
cymbal ⎪
bass drum ⎪
xylophone ⎪
bells ⎪
chimes ⎬ 3 players
gong ⎪
tamborine ⎪
castanets ⎪
triangle ⎪
etc. ⎭

A fifth section of special instruments that don't fit the above categories should be added:

piano, harpsichord, celesta and organ—1 player
harp—2 players

Thus, an orchestra using six French horns will number 102 players. Some orchestras reduce the number of strings somewhat below the seventy players we outlined. For certain music additional players will be brought in, making the group even larger.

A number of seating arrangements are possible but the two most common ones are those shown on page 18.

The Strings

The strings give the orchestra its special character (in contrast to the various types of bands where strings are generally not used at all). They constitute better than two thirds of the group in order

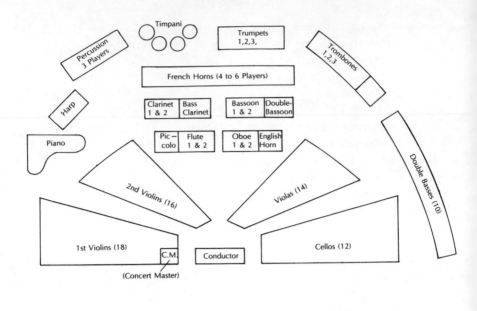

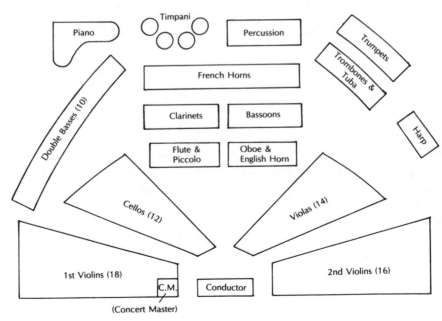

18

to balance the stronger tones of the winds and brasses. All the stringed instruments are capable of all the techniques and effects we attributed to the violin when we were discussing tone color.

The first violin section is usually the highest voice (soprano) in the string section and is often given the lushest melodies. There is a distinctive sonority to eighteen violins playing the same melody in unison—altogether different from the sound of a solo violin. When the composer requires a solo violin, the most competent player, who sits in the first chair of the section and is called the concertmaster, plays the part. The concertmaster is also responsible for seeing that all eighteen first violinists bow together, and it is he who tunes the orchestra. Next to him sits the assistant concertmaster, who plays secondary solos.

The second violins sometimes join the firsts in reinforcing a melody, but more often they lend a supporting harmonic background or play a countermelody. There is no technical difference between a first and second violin. The instruments are identical. Only the parts they are assigned to play are different. And since the second violin parts are the less showy of the two, we have made this comparison part of our everyday speech by referring to anyone who is overshadowed by another as "playing second fiddle." Yet without the second violin the orchestral sound would be less rich and full. As in every team, all the players are important, not just the quarterback or the home run hitter.

The violas are simply enlarged violins, held in the same playing position and played with the same techniques. However, the larger size produces lower pitches and a less brilliant tone. Like the second violins, they generally lend harmonic support, but when they emerge in a melody the tone is "darker" than that of the violins. They are the altos of the string section.

The cellos are the tenors of the string section, but these voice classifications must not be taken too literally because all the string instruments have ranges wider than vocal ranges. Consequently, the cello frequently reaches up into the high soprano ranges.

The cello is much larger than the violin or viola and so is held

19

between the knees as the player sits. Like the first violin, it is frequently given important melodic passages, where its lower range of pitches gives its tone quality a warmth and depth in contrast to the greater brilliance and shimmer of the violins. When it doesn't have a melodic function, it joins the basses in providing the foundation for the whole musical structure, the very fundamental bass part.

The basses are even larger than the cellos and require the players to stand or use a high stool. They produce the lowest pitches in the string section and thus support all the harmony produced above. Occasionally they venture forth in a melodic passage where the effect is usually mysterious, foreboding or sometimes stately and often ponderous.

Sometimes, for a very dramatic or very passionate effect, a composer will use all the strings in unison (or octaves); seventy strings playing the same thing can have terrific impact.

Like the first violins, each section has its most competent player in the first seat, and he is called principal player or leader of the particular section. He is responsible for seeing that everyone bows together and for playing any solo passages for his instrument.

The Woodwinds

This family of instruments is sometimes referred to as "reeds" which gives us a clue to their origin. When they were mostly fashioned from the hollow wood reeds like cane and bamboo, holes were burned or drilled into a length of hollow cane producing a primitive flute. Today, we use fine woods and metals and a variety of mouthpieces, shapes and sizes to produce a number of very versatile instruments.

The modern flute, and its half-size version, the piccolo, are now made of metal (nickel or silver or gold or platinum). The tone is produced by blowing across an open hole in much the same way as one can produce a sound by blowing across the top of an empty Coca-Cola bottle. Pitch is changed by opening and closing holes along the length of the instrument. The flute tone is clear and birdlike while the piccolo, higher in pitch, is shrill and piercing. The flute is capable of long, sustained melodic passages and both instruments can execute very rapid technical passages.

The oboe is related to the oriental snake charmer's pipe and to the bagpipe. It is played through a mouthpiece consisting of two almost paper-thin slivers of cane fastened to a tiny pipe. The player must force air past the two pieces of cane into the pipe and thence through the instrument. The two pieces are thus forced to vibrate which produces the oboe tone and classifies the oboe as a double reed instrument. The slightly nasal, penetrating quality of the oboe sound is effectively used in long melodies, especially plaintive ones, but it, too, can run with the rest of the orchestra.

The English horn is an alto oboe and is neither English nor a horn. The story goes that its name is the result of a printer's mistake. The English horn bears the same relationship to the oboe as does the viola to the violin. It produces a darker, moodier sound than the oboe, but is capable of all the same techniques. Oboes and English horns are made of wood.

The clarinet is the most mellifluous of the woodwinds, but it can also be shrill and strident or heavy and ponderous. Its tone is produced by a single reed or thin piece of cane that vibrates against a mouthpiece. It is an extremely agile instrument and frequently sparkles with flashy effects in jazz. It is generally made of wood though it can be made of metal and it comes in several sizes. In addition to the standard Bb and A sizes which are used interchangeably, the orchestra occasionally uses a small Eb clarinet (higher in pitch, and, like the piccolo, piercing in tone) and the bass clarinet, larger and much lower in pitch. There is also an alto clarinet, slightly lower in pitch, a little larger in size, and less frequently used.

While not regular members of the orchestra, saxophones are sometimes "borrowed" from the "pop music" world. They are single reed instruments, like the clarinet, but are always made of metal and come in a variety of sizes (ranges). They tend to overpower the other woodwinds and the strings which is why they are less common in orchestras than in bands.

The bassoon is sometimes called the "clown" of the orchestra, because it can produce a kind of buzzy tone which can be very funny in the lower registers, but it can also be plaintive and tender and quite exotic in the same tenor range as the cello. It is a double reed instrument, like the oboe, but much larger in size. The double bassoon or contrabassoon is larger and lower still.

The woodwinds are usually paired (first and second flute, first and second oboe, first and second clarinet and first and second bassoon) with the addition of piccolo, English horn, extra clarinets and double bassoon as needed. The pairs most often play different parts—that is first flute will play a part different from second flute and so on down the line. When all the woodwinds do play together in unison or in sustained chordal harmony the sound is somewhat like that of an organ.

The Brasses

The brass instruments found their way into the modern symphony orchestra somewhat more slowly than the woodwinds. In their simplest and earliest forms they were only able to produce the few notes of a bugle call. Later the invention of the slide permitted the trombone and the trumpet to produce more notes. And then, in the nineteenth century, the invention of valves enabled all the brasses to produce all the notes. Both slide and valves were means of extending the length of tubing in the instrument thus increasing its range and the number of notes it could play. All brass instruments have a cup-shaped mouthpiece. The player places his lips against this cup and forces breath through them with a buzzing sound. He controls the pitch by tightening his lips for high sounds and loosening them for low ones.

The French horn appears frequently in seventeenth and eighteenth century orchestras, limiting itself to the few notes of the bugle or hunting horn calls. In fact, at that time, the instrument was a true hunting horn. Later it appears with greater frequency and in increasing numbers as the valves increase its musical possibilities. The French horn tone quality blends readily with other instruments so that it is often used in harmonic combinations with the woodwinds and the strings as well as with the brasses. It can play extended melodies with a hauntingly lovely and gentle character or be aggressively military or stentorian. When muted, it becomes mean and nasty or spooky and mysterious. It has an extremely wide range which makes mastery of the instrument very difficult.

The trumpet also appears in the early orchestras and in rather demanding technical parts which seem to be beyond the possibilities of the early instruments, as in the *Brandenburg Concertos* of Bach. But research reveals that these parts were played on specially built small instruments which produced the brilliant, high pitch and were played by virtuosi skilled in forcing out with their lips notes not normally found on the instrument. These parts are much more playable on the modern valved instrument. The trumpet, too, has its lyric moments, but more often serves in its brassy, brilliant, forceful style. Hence a fanfare is defined as a "flourish of trumpets" and has come to mean a showy display.

The trombone is the "heavy" of the orchestra. It produces a big sound in the baritone range and so is identified with virile and masculine qualities. But it can be sweet and tender, too, and sometimes very funny when the slide is used to produce special effects. Trombones are now also made with valves, but most trombonists prefer the slide. The bass trombone is slightly larger and has an extended lower range.

The tuba is the "grandaddy" of the brasses (and of the orchestra) and can be grumpy, mysterious, gentle or just plain low. It, like the other low register instruments already described, serves as a foundation for the total orchestral sound.

Miscellaneous other brasses make occasional appearances in the orchestra. The cornet is much like the trumpet, but slightly mellower in sound. It appears regularly in symphonic bands. The baritone or euphonium is much like the trombone in range, but again, mellower in sound. It looks like a small tuba. It, too, is very important in bands.

Richard Wagner created a whole set of instruments for his own music called "Wagner tubas" which are really more like French horns than tubas and which add still another quality or tone color to the brass choir.

The entire brass section, when used as a unit, is capable of producing overwhelmingly powerful sound. It can also temper this strength and blend it into effects of quiet dignity and solemnity.

The Percussion Instruments

Percussion instruments are instruments which produce sound by being struck or hit; for most of us this means drums. There are, however, many other kinds of percussion instruments. Contrary to the popular belief that "almost anyone can play the drums" a good percussionist must be a superbly trained musician. He must develop different techniques for the various instruments. His understanding and feeling for rhythm must be precise and acute. And since many of these instruments are pitched and some must be tuned while the whole orchestra is playing, his ear must be critical and exacting.

The percussion section is sometimes referred to as "the Battery" with some poetic justice, because a great deal of orchestral "fireworks" is generated here. But this is only a small part of the picture.

The timpani or kettledrums are the most frequently used percussion instruments in the symphony orchestra and therefore have a player specially assigned to them. They are always used in pairs, so at least two and often four are visible on the stage. They are huge copper bowls over which skin is stretched in such a way that it can be tightened or loosened, thus changing the pitch. The timpanist must often tune them while music swirls about him. The skins are struck with mallets with heads of varying degrees of hardness. Rhythms can reach terrifying degrees of complexity and with all this, the timpanist must be able to exert sufficient control to produce a barely audible heartbeat or a deafening thunderclap. All symphonic percussionists are capable of handling all the instruments including the timpani, but the most prestigious player is the timpanist.

The rest of the instruments in this grouping are handled by the other players in the section with one musician frequently playing several different instruments in the same selection. This is possible because these are "special effect" instruments and some may be used for only one note in the entire work.

Borrowed from the military band are the bass and snare drums and the cymbal. The bass drum is the large drum which appears in the marching band on the belly of the player, supported by straps across his shoulders. It is struck alternately on each side by two large mallets with padded heads. It produces a booming sound. The snare drum is smaller and hangs at an angle across the hips and thighs of the marching player. It is struck only on the top skin by wooden sticks and produces a kind of rattling sound created by strings of metal or gut stretched across the underskin which vibrate against it. Of course, in the orchestra, both instruments are supported on stands with the players standing behind them. The cymbals are two large plates of spun or hammered brass that are crashed together with varying degrees of force. A single cymbal is sometimes suspended from a stand and played with drum sticks.

Another grouping of percussion instruments can produce the full scale of pitches. These include the xylophone, bells, chimes, etc.

The xylophone is a series of wooden bars of graduated lengths arranged to produce all the notes of the scale. It is played with wooden or plastic mallets and is capable of almost all the melodic and harmonic effects of a piano, except that its tone is brittle like "rattling bones." Saint-Saëns uses it for precisely this effect in *Danse Macabre*. The orchestral bells or *glockenspiel* is played the same way only the bars are metal instead of wood, and the tone is bell–like instead of bonelike. The chimes are a series of chrome (or silver or gold) tubes of graduated lengths hung vertically from a rack and struck with a hammerlike mallet. They look like a display of vertically hung towel bars, but they produce the sound of church bells in all the pitches of the scale.

Then there is a whole host of special atmospheric instruments that immediately summon up a particular locale or an ethnic flavor.

the Oriental gong—a big brass plate struck with a soft mallet
that signals the entrance of the sultan or the Chinese emperor.

the tambourine—a tiny half-drum with metal jangles mounted on its sides that is shaken and struck by hand and immediately suggests Italian folk dancing.

castanets—two shallow wooden cups tied together and held so that they can be clicked together by motion of the thumb and fingers. The effect is instantaneously Spanish.

the triangle—a metal bar bent into the shape of a triangle and struck with another metal bar. The resulting "ping" can penetrate and sharpen even a heavy orchestral texture, but when used delicately can produce a gossamer, fairy tale effect.

There are literally hundreds of such instruments—maracas and claves from Latin America, bongo drums from Africa, tom-toms from the American Indian—just too many to include here. Sometimes composers call for special effects mechanically or realistically produced. Such things as wind machines, water tanks, typewriters, bird whistles, recordings of bird calls, and even a cannon have at one time or another fallen to the lot of the percussionist.

Some instruments don't fit neatly into the classifications discussed here, but appear with some frequency in the orchestra.

The harpsichord which is very much a part of the seventeenth and eighteenth century orchestra is a plectrum (plucked) instrument as well as a stringed instrument, since its strings are picked by wooden or leather jacks activated from a keyboard.

The harp is also a plucked instrument (although plectra or picks are not used). Harps are usually used in pairs since they involve a rather elaborate pedal technique and in much music must play alternately so that one musician can reset the pedals while the other plays.

The piano produces its tone through a keyboard with hammers (percussion) but, like the harpsichord and the harp, it is also a stringed instrument.

The celesta is really a set of orchestral bells provided with a resonating box and a keyboard and rightfully belongs in the percussion section, but since it involves a keyboard it is usually played by a pianist. Like its name, its effect is "celestial."

The organ originally was basically a woodwind instrument, since its pipes usually contained metal reeds and often some of the pipes themselves were made of wood. But it, too, is a keyboard instrument and, today, frequently has no pipes at all but produces its sound electronically, so its classification is, to say the least, confused.

*   *   *

You have just been presented with a large list of instruments, all too briefly described, that comprise the modern orchestra. You are undoubtedly familiar with some of them. The next time you listen to an orchestra try to single out the instruments you are familiar with, even if the violin is the only stringed instrument you are sure of and the trumpet the only brass. When you are practiced enough to be sure of these, you can try others. A number of recordings are designed to help you recognize instruments and some illustrate the instruments, show how they are held and how big they are in relation to the players and each other.* If you can watch rehearsals of a school or community orchestra you will learn to recognize the instruments very quickly. You will also get an insight into many other aspects of making music and of listening.

---

* Recordings for recognition of instruments are not usually listed in general record catalogues, so we list three here:
1. INSTRUMENTS OF THE ORCHESTRA
   RCA Victor LES-6000—National Symphony Orchestra with Howard Mitchell
   (two records with illustrated and informative printed manual, each instrument on a separate band)
2. INSTRUMENTS OF THE ORCHESTRA
   Vanguard VSD 721/22-Vienna State Opera Orchestra with David Randolph
   (two records, each instrument on a separate band, no pictures)
3. THE SERAPHIM GUIDE TO THE INSTRUMENTS OF THE ORCHESTRA
   Seraphim S-60234—London Philharmonic Orchestra with Sir Adrian Boult
   (one record, one band for each family of instruments, no pictures)

IV

THE CONDUCTOR

Every member of a professional symphony orchestra is a highly trained musician, an artist in his own right. He may have ideas about the music the orchestra is playing that differ somewhat from those of the player next to him. "This passage should be played more slowly. We're getting too loud too fast. The tone quality of the strings should be more warm and tender (more *vibrato*) etc., etc." With a hundred players there could be a hundred different conceptions. Even though the composer very carefully indicates exactly what he wants in terms of notes, rhythms, dynamics, mood and tempo, the performer has considerable leeway in interpreting his directions. In large groups, if each player were free to follow his own ideas the results would be chaotic. It is the job of the conductor to prevent such chaos and to mold the performance so that it projects a unified conception of the music.

To do this, the conductor must first be a musician of such great talent that all the great talents in the orchestra can look up to him with respect. And since it will be his interpretation that must finally prevail, he must be both tactful and strong, diplomatic and forceful. Musicians like any other people, can be jealous, competitive, hostile. Orchestras can be riddled with rivalries. But our great conductors are held in such awe by the players that a cohesive team effort is achieved. Some conductors are dictatorial martinets and are feared and even hated by their orchestras. Others are benign autocrats and are loved. But either way, the conductor has the final say on all musical matters and must have the authority and musicianship to make it stick.

If you are fortunate enough to be able to see a great conductor in

"Delicately, please."

live performance (and this is frequently possible on television), you will, if you are observant, be treated to what can best be described as a guided tour through the music he is conducting. His right hand essentially beats time and holds the orchestra together rhythmically. He may or may not use a baton (a thin, light stick). His left hand is used to communicate dynamic effects, to bring out melodic lines, to shape musical phrases, to cue in instruments, to balance the total sound by subduing certain instruments and encouraging others. But both hands must be able to do both jobs interchangeably if necessary. And the conductor's face, especially his eyes, can reveal much of the mood and message of the music. So can the stance of his body as he moves from a crouch to a fully erect position to produce a gradual *crescendo*. A toss of the head for a triumphant flourish, the set of the shoulders for a belligerent passage, the closing of the eyes for a prayerful interlude—all these and more are the conductor's stock in trade. He must be a great silent communicator, an actor

"More *first violin.*"

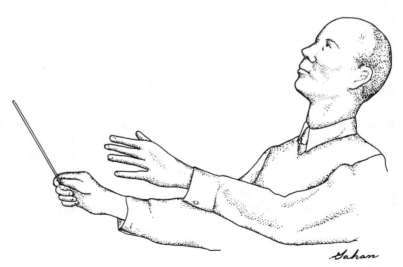

"*Prayerfully.*"

gifted in the art of pantomime, a dancer of sorts. He must also be a great teacher, able to communicate ideas verbally in rehearsal.

The conductor is the program maker. He must understand public taste and when and how to cater to it. However, he also has an obligation to composers, new and old. If he is not willing to introduce new works or to rediscover neglected but worthy old ones, music as an art would begin to stagnate. So he must use his experience and judgment in assessing and developing new talents. Sometimes he will run counter to his audience's preference, and this takes courage since his job depends on his ability to attract the paying customers. Leonard Bernstein once announced a difficult modern work which was received with mixed reactions by the audience, many of whom walked out. In spite of this, feeling the work was too difficult to understand at one hearing, he immediately played it again.

Not only must he make each individual program varied and interesting, but, if he is the permanent conductor of the orchestra, he must plan the whole season's programs in such a way that anyone subscribing to a series of concerts will find no duplication, no overstressing of any one type of music and enough new and enough old to hold his interest.

Therefore, the conductor must have the broadest background in music of all periods, types, moods, nationalities, etc. He must know them well enough to conduct them. Nowadays it is fashionable to conduct from memory and this requires even more study than conducting with the music (score). The score itself is most complicated to read, let alone memorize, since it includes all the separate parts for all the individual instruments and sections of the orchestra. Frequently the conductor is reading thirty to forty separate parts simultaneously and his ear must be sharp enough to pick out and correct mistakes in such a complex texture of sound. His repertory in a single season may comprise several hundred compositions.

Since he sets the interpretive and artistic standards for the orchestra, the conductor must have a thorough knowledge of the technical workings and possibilities of all the instruments of the orchestra. This does not mean he has to be able to play them, but

Page of score (conductor's music) from last movement of Scheherezade *calling for thirty-one separate parts to be read simultaneously.*

he must know what they can do easily and well, what is difficult for them, and what they cannot be called upon to do. Sometimes composers, who should, but don't always have this knowledge, write impossible parts, and the conductor must be sufficiently aware of this to ask the composer (if he is alive and available) to revise the parts, or else be able to make the revisions himself. This technical knowledge is also important in the hiring (and firing) of members of the orchestra, for this is usually the conductor's responsibility. It is he who must judge the overall ability of new players, keep tabs on the continuing proficiency of old members and arrange their placement in the group according to ability.

Orchestral conductors frequently work with choruses and vocal soloists or conduct opera, and so they must also be familiar with voices and vocal techniques. The reverse is true, though less frequently, of choral conductors who occasionally take over an orchestra. Usually, though, the choral director is more specialized and will train the chorus which will then perform with orchestra under the leadership of the orchestral conductor.

Small wonder that with such demands on his talent, the conductor who makes the grade is a star.

V

THE VIRTUOSO

In the visual arts and literature the artist or writer creates and the audience sees or reads, but in music the composer reaches his audience through a performer. Thus, communication is through a third person (or persons) and not as direct as in painting or sculpture or in a novel or essay. Just as in the theatre where two actors can interpret the same role and deliver the same lines quite differently, so two performing musicians can play the same music with totally different effect. Of course, the notes and rhythms and, for the most part, the dynamics will be as the composer wrote them, but like the symphony orchestra conductor, each performer has his own interpretation.

Performers also vary in their technical expertise. The composer tries to write music that can be played by a proficient performer. However, when Tchaikovsky brought his *First Piano Concerto* to Nicholas Rubinstein, himself a composer and teacher and a very great pianist, Rubinstein declared the work unplayable. Undaunted, Tchaikovsky took the work to Hans von Bülow, another outstanding pianist of the day, who mastered it and performed it. Today any concert pianist worthy of the name is able to play this concerto and many works even more difficult. Sometimes it is the performer himself whose skill is so great that he demands ever greater technical challenges. Paganini, an early nineteenth century violinist, had such prodigious skill that very few existing compositions even began to utilize it. So he wrote a great deal of music for the violin himself. This music was full of the difficult tricks and flashy passages of which he alone was capable. But it wasn't long after Paganini introduced these techniques that other violinists mastered them and other composers wrote them into their music.

34

And so it runs in a kind of never ending succession. Composers make new demands on the technical skills of performers and soon the performers rise to meet them. Then the performers develop skills beyond what anyone has yet written and composers are soon calling for these newest skills.

Sometimes the mechanical improvement of an instrument increases its musical possibilities. There is no doubt that the great violins fashioned by Amati, Guarneri and Stradivari went far to improve the quality of violin playing as did the introduction of a better bow designed by Tourte. The invention of sophisticated key systems greatly expanded the techniques of the woodwinds, while the application of the valve system to the brasses did the same thing.

When a performer achieves an outstanding level of skills both technical and interpretive he is called a virtuoso. Audiences delight in virtuosity. The listener can derive great pleasure and excitement from the apparently effortless speed with which the violinist or pianist tears off an intricate and devilishly difficult passage. It sounds so easy and so perfect. We respond to the warm rich tone, to the carefully graded dynamic changes, to the rhythm that drives and pulses, to the long melodic line that floats on a breath that never gives out and to the overall build-up to real climaxes. A true virtuoso not only plays to but plays with his listeners, sweeping them along in his own frenzy, saddening them with his own grief, driving them with his own urgency, calming them with his own peace. You may say that all this is in the music and that the composer put it there, and of course you are right. But so often the performer fails to communicate it or communicates it so that calm becomes dull, urgent becomes nervous, and sad becomes maudlin. And where speed and technical difficulty are involved, the inadequate artist gets so involved with just negotiating the correct notes that his performance becomes purely mechanical and communicates nothing at all. Some artists achieve prodigious mechanical skill, but fail to develop interpretively. They are not virtuosos. One must be outstanding in all aspects of his performing art to qualify.

In the seventeenth and eighteenth centuries, musicians developed many skills. Mozart performed proficiently on the violin, viola and

35

piano and often appeared as soloist in his own concertos. Even today composing and performing sometimes go hand in hand. But virtuosity has risen to such high and demanding levels that the virtuoso has become very much a specialist and few indeed are the composers who can meet today's performing standards.

VI

POETRY AND MUSIC
SONG (FOLK AND ART)
SMALL FORMS

One of the oldest forms of music is the song and our earliest poets were singers. The Psalms of the Bible were sung or recited by David to the accompaniment of the psaltery, a kind of harp. Much history and even news of the day was handed down and transmitted by the poet-musicians of ancient times. We call them bards or minstrels. The music served to heighten or reinforce the effect of the words and also made them easier to remember. (You may have noticed how, when you recall the melody of a song, the words frequently fall right in place.) As writing and printing developed the roles of poet and musician separated. Today, composers usually select poems that move them and create songs, although in the realm of "pop" music there has been a resurgence of poet-musicians.

Naturally, when words are used with music, little is left to the imagination of the listener. The message or meaning of the song comes across quite clearly through the words. The music personalizes the meaning, giving the listener the special reactions of the composer.

There are many types and classifications of songs, but we will concern ourselves mainly with two—the folk song and the art song.

Folk music is literally music of the people. It grew out of the necessity of the uneducated and unskilled to give expression to their interests and emotions in song and dance. Since music notation was

37

at first undeveloped and the people largely illiterate until the nineteenth century, this music (and poetry) was handed down orally from generation to generation. It dealt with universal subjects such as work, love, children, the seasons, home, religion, the native land and so on. It was strongly ethnic in character—that is, recognizably French, Spanish, Italian, German, Negro, English, etc. In America, where settlers and immigrants represent so many cultures, we find many folk styles and influences. Since so much of this music was transmitted orally, there are no signed original manuscripts and so composers are hard to trace. This gives rise to the idea that folk music has no composers. Occasionally one does come across music that might have been generated spontaneously by a group, such as a work song sung by a chain gang. Perhaps a line was sung by one prisoner, then picked up by the group and chanted and elaborated on, or a "revival" shout uttered by someone at a religious meeting might, in the same way, be developed into a spiritual. For the most part, however, a folk song, both words and music, is the work of one individual who didn't and probably couldn't write it down. As a result, he seldom sang it twice exactly the same way, and as his friends picked it up, they, too, made little changes, both in words and tune. After a while under such circumstances, it becomes difficult to pin down the origin.

Folk songs tend to be rhythmic, with simple tunes, and rather repetitious, and so they are easy to learn and rermember. As one studies them, certain patterns of repetition can be noticed. *On Top of Old Smoky* is a one sentence song, where each verse or stanza is one sentence long, and the same tune is repeated for each verse. *Oh My Darling Clementine* also uses one tune for each verse (consisting of a longer sentence than *Old Smoky* or sometimes two short ones) and repeats the tune for its refrain as well. (See examples 1 and 2.)

America (*My Country 'tis of Thee*), our version of the British national anthem, is a two part song with a first tune comprising the words "My country 'tis of thee, sweet land of liberty, of thee I sing." The second tune sets the words "Land where my fathers died, Land of the Pilgrim's pride, From every mountainside, let freedom ring."

On Top of Old Smoky

On top of old Smok - y____ All cov - ered with snow____
____ I lost my true lov - er____ come a court - ing too slow.____

Oh My Darling Clementine

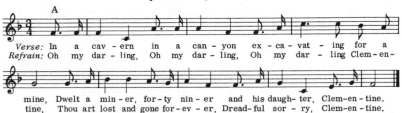

Verse: In a cav - ern in a can - yon ex - ca - vat - ing for a
Refrain: Oh my dar - ling, Oh my dar - ling, Oh my dar - ling Clem - en-

mine, Dwelt a min - er, for - ty nin - er and his daugh - ter, Clem-en - tine.
tine, Thou art lost and gone for - ev - er, Dread - ful sor - ry, Clem-en - tine.

America

My coun - try 'tis of thee, Sweet land of lib - er - ty,
Of thee I sing; Land where my fa - thers died! Land of the
Pil - grim's pride! From ev - 'ry__ moun - tain side, Let__ free - dom ring.

Since the two tunes are different we can designate the first as "A" and the second as "B." *America* therefore is a two part song whose pattern or form can be expressed as AB (see example 3). *Old Smoky* and *Clementine* having only one tune each, would be represented as A, A, A etc.

Now let's analyze the tune structure of *Deck the Halls,* a traditional Christmas carol. The first tune covers "Deck the halls with

39

boughs of holly, fa la la la la fa la la la." The same tune is repeated for " 'Tis the season to be jolly, fa la la la la fa la la la." A new tune is introduced for "Don we now our gay apparel, fa la la, fa la la, la la la." Then the first tune returns for "Troll the ancinet Yuletide carol, fa la la la la, fa la la la." Thus we have AABA (see example 4). We refer to this form, in which the first melody returns after a

Deck the Halls

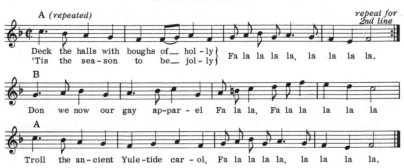

contrasting middle part, as a three part form. It is one of the most used patterns in music and serves as the standard pattern for most popular songs. Because it repeats its first tune, it provides for ready recognition and remembering, and recognition is one of the great pleasures of listening. In later chapters we shall see how this little three part pattern is expanded into much larger forms.

Other forms are possible. If you analyze *The Star Spangled Banner* you will discover its pattern is AABC. But it is enough for now if you understand that musical form is based on the way in which musical ideas are ordered. And this system evolved in its simplest form from folk music.

Some music by well known composers is really folk music because it succeeds in achieving a folk style or a traditional quality. The songs of Stephen Foster, Handel's *Joy to the World*, Brahms' *Lullaby*, *America* and *Silent Night* are examples.

The art song is the work of a composer who selects a poem that he feels he can "illuminate" with his music. It can, like the folk song, repeat the same melody for each verse in which case we say it is a strophic song. The form of the melody for each verse may be any of those already described. But, unlike the folk song, which is generally unaccompanied or accompanied by a simple chordal background on a guitar, the art song has a carefully written and coordinated accompaniment designed to underscore some of the ideas of the text. Most songs call for a piano accompaniment, but various instrumental combinations from string trio to full symphony orchestra can be and have been used. Schubert, in a strophic song called *The Trout* writes a melody of folk songlike simplicity, but the piano accompaniment ripples along in a remarkably successful description of the fast flowing brook in which the trout swims.

The art song can also depart from any set pattern of melodic repetition and instead have the music follow the text so closely that each line has its unique setting. Such a song is called "through composed," and an example is Schubert's *Erlking* described in Chapter II in the section on tone color. Schubert changes the melody for each change in "point of view" in the poem. When the poet asks "Who rides so late through night and wind? It is a father and his child!," the accompaniment drives forward like a galloping horse with rumblings of thunder in the background. When the Erlking (Death) invites the child to go with him, the music becomes sweetly seductive and the driving accompaniment relaxes (but without losing momentum) into a sort of harplike style. When the child, in his delirium reacts in fear, a note of terror and hysteria creeps into the melody and agitation returns to the accompaniment. This is carried into the father's anguished and desperate efforts to comfort the child. The intensity increases until the wild ride ends with dramatic abruptness. "The child was dead!" In the space of a few minutes Schubert and Goethe, the poet, have created a complete theatre piece for four characters—the poet-narrator, the father, the child and the Erlking. One singer projects all four parts, giving them individual characterizations to the best of his ability while the accompaniment supplies all the lighting effects and scenery through its vivid depiction of the stormy night. Rarely has a story been told more effectively and concisely than in the words and music of this brief masterpiece.

41

The art song, too, has a long history with many distinguished examples stemming from the sixteenth, seventeenth and eighteenth centuries and from all the countries of the Western world. But in the nineteenth century, especially in Germany, this form really blossomed. The idealism fostered by the American and French revolutions, the individualism and emotionalism that characterized the newly emerging and prosperous middle classes all found expression in the works of the great German poets Goethe, Schiller and Heine and others. These in turn fired the imaginations of composers like Beethoven, Schubert, Mendelssohn, Schumann and Brahms. The development of the piano gave further challenge to the composers for here was a worthy partner for the voice, fuller toned and capable of a greater variety of effects than any of the instruments previously available for accompaniments. Schubert was particularly fond of the *"lied,"* as the German art song was called, and wrote hundreds of them. When a number of songs dealt with the same general subject and were intended to be sung in sequence, they were called a song-cycle. Schubert's *Wintereise* (*Winter's Journey*) and Schumann's *Dichterliebe* (*Poet's Love*) are examples.

The song forms (sometimes called short forms) are by no means limited to vocal music. Mendelssohn, in addition to writing many songs, wrote a whole set of piano pieces called *Songs Without Words* all of which can be analyzed as simply as the two and three part folk songs we've already explored. However, without words we must depend entirely on our ability to remember and recognize melodies for this analysis, and this requires more concentration. These forms also strongly influenced longer and more ambitious vocal and instrumental works, as we shall see. By itself the great art song is a gem—not a big flashy stone, but a perfectly polished miniature—a sentimental and personal treasure.

VII

DRAMA AND MUSIC
OPERA, BALLET, AND ORATORIO

The combination of words and music finds its most elaborate expression in opera. An opera is a fully staged play in which all the characters sing their parts, often with full orchestral accompaniment, instead of speaking them. Opera is a descendant of the great Greek plays of antiquity, where dance, ritual, choral chanting and a highly poetic and declamatory style of speaking (almost singing) all combined to provide a performance sufficiently impressive for the important religious festivals of which they were a part. Opera also borrowed from the miracle and morality plays of the Middle Ages and from the elaborate court entertainments (masques and spectacles) of the great European monarchs such as Louis XIV and Catherine the Great. The result is a form of drama that demands a great deal of its audience. In the first place people just don't sing their everyday conversations, so one begins by accepting a strange and artificial situation. Secondly, unlike in song, where the communication seems intimate and direct, in opera the communication is between characters on the stage and is supported by a symphony orchestra, a large chorus and a corps de ballet. Opera plots, therefore, tend to deal with the spectacular and heroic. Even when the plots are more realistic, they deal with the strongest emotions and most violent passions. In lighter moods, the comedy is broad and sometimes effective use is made of fantasy and the supernatural. But seldom is opera really believable. When it marshalls all its forces, however, it can be overwhelmingly powerful, touchingly romantic, superbly dramatic and gripping and truly grand. This is why, although it is enormously costly to produce and tickets are outrageously expensive, grand opera endures.

The beginnings of opera, as we know it today, date back to the seventeenth century in Italy, but most of the standard repertoire of modern opera companies consists largely of nineteenth century works with some eighteenth and twentieth century operas included. The largest number of these are Italian operas, but there are a good number of German and French works and some Russian and English. In America it is the general practice to sing the opera in the language in which it was written. Lately, there has been some pressure to use English translations. In Europe, operas are usually translated into the language of the country where the performance takes place. The American listener, therefore, is at a disadvantage compared to his European counterpart, since he most often is listening to a language he may not understand. It can be argued that even when one knows the language many passages in opera are difficult to understand because the melodic line is too florid, syllables are extended over many notes, duets, trios and quartets are frequent with each singer uttering different words at the same time, and sometimes the chorus adds to the verbal confusion.

How, then, does the listener approach opera? Slowly, and a little at a time. It is obvious that if one does not understand the language it is necessary to find out what's being sung. It is also clear that a long three hour performance in a foreign language takes quite a bit of finding out. It is better, therefore, to limit oneself at first to the highlights of some of the most loved and most popular operas. These operas have moments that have become so well known that they are frequently performed as separate selections in concert or on the air. The *Toreador Song* from *Carmen*, the *Triumphal March* from *Aïda*, Figaro's song, *Largo al Factotum*, from *The Barber of Seville* are a few examples. They appeal to us because they are melodically attractive and because they offer a showcase for a great voice, or in the *Aïda* selection, for massed voices.

Let us take a "highlight" look at the opera *Carmen* by Georges Bizet, certainly one of the most frequently performed operas in the repertoire. You can use almost any recording or tape labeled *Selections, Highlights* or *Hits* from *Carmen,* but make sure that it is a vocal recording by reputable artists. (Avoid the many such records where the vocal parts are arranged for orchestra and no singing is involved.) On it you will find most, if not all, of the selections described.

Carmen is a French opera about a Spanish gypsy girl. It takes place in and around Seville in the latter half of the nineteenth century.

Act I—A square in Seville

Micaela, a young girl from the country, asks the soldiers on guard duty the whereabouts of Corporal Don José, her fiancé. She leaves when they flirt with her. The guard changes and Don José comes on with the new group and a crowd of little children imitating the soldiers and singing a marching song. Meanwhile a nearby cigarette factory empties for lunch and among the female workers is the beautiful but fickle Carmen who is attracted to the handsome José and attempts to charm him with the familiar and seductive *Habanera,* a song in a tangolike rhythm in which she describes love as a "wild bird that none may tame." As the crowd watches, amused, she throws him a rose. The workers, including Carmen, return to the factory, and Micaela reenters with a letter for José from his mother. This gives rise to a lovely *Duet* about home and mother but it is evident that José has been deeply disturbed by Carmen. As Micaela leaves, the girls from the factory pour forth in great excitement over a fight between Carmen and a co-worker who charges Carmen with assault. Carmen is arrested, her hands bound, and she is left in the charge of José while his lieutenant, Zuniga, goes off to arrange the necessary papers. Again, Carmen goes to work on José, this time in hope of gaining her freedom by promising him her love. She sings the *Seguidilla,* in Spanish dance rhythm, telling how she will dance for him if he will meet her at the inn of Lillas Pastia outside of Seville. José succumbs. He loosens her bonds and she escapes. He is sent to prison for two months for letting her get away.

45

Outside cigarette factory. Act I, Carmen

Act II—*The Inn of Lillas Pastia*

The second act opens with a gay *Gypsy Song and Dance* led by Carmen that grows ever faster and wilder as it goes, revealing something of the recklessness of Carmen's nature. She is awaiting Don

46

José who is this day released from prison, but while she waits, Escamillo, the great toreador (bullfighter), arrives. He sings his famous *Toreador Song* in which he describes the excitement, tension, courage and triumph the bullfighter feels in the arena. He is

At the Inn of Lillas Pastia. Act II, Carmen

much taken with Carmen and midway in his song he mentions the rewards that await him after the fight. Among them is love. But Carmen, at least for the moment, loves José who went to jail so she could go free. Escamillo leaves. Some of the gypsies are smugglers and in a wonderful *Quintet* four of them conspire with Carmen to get José to join them as a smuggler. José arrives and is left alone

47

with Carmen. To the accompaniment of castanets she dances for him, but he is distracted by the bugle sounding in the distance calling him to duty. She laughs at him for preferring army life to life with her. To prove his love he takes from his tunic the rose she had thrown him two months earlier (in Act I), and sings the touching, almost pathetic *Flower Song* telling how this flower and the thought of meeting her tonight helped him through his imprisonment. They are interrupted by Zuniga who flirts with Carmen and orders José back to the barracks. In a jealous rage, José attacks Zuniga. The smugglers break up the fight, but now José, having attacked his superior, has no choice but to join the smugglers.

Act III—*The Mountain Headquarters of the Smugglers*

Carmen and José quarrel. She has obviously tired of him and he, now an outlaw and deserter, cannot return to his former life. Carmen turns to the cards to tell her fortune and that of two of her gypsy friends. In this *Card Song* the girls foresee handsome and rich lovers and their music is light and happy, but Carmen foresees only death and her music provides a dramatic and somber contrast. Micaela, seeking José, enters and in a beautiful song (*Micaela's Aria*) voices her fears at being alone in the mountains and tries to summon up the courage to face José and Carmen. Escamillo also arrives, seeking Carmen, and inevitably he and the jealous José fight, but are separated by the smugglers. Micaela tells José his mother is dying, and while Escamillo invites Carmen and her friends to his next bullfight, José leaves with Micaela promising Carmen she has not seen the last of him.

Act IV—*Outside the Bullring in Seville*

Festive music and rousing choruses greet Escamillo, escorting Carmen, as he arrives for the bullfight. There is a short love duet (*Si tu m'aimes*) between the two and Escamillo and the crowd enter the ring while Carmen remains outside. She has seen José in the crowd and is determined finally to free herself of him. He is just as determined not to give her up. He promises to do anything for her. She wants only freedom. What's more, she now loves Escamillo. At this point the cheers for Escamillo's triumph are heard from within the arena. In a fury, José stabs Carmen as she tries to run into the arena, just as Escamillo and the crowd emerge to see José weeping over the body of the Carmen he loved and killed. This *Finale* is one of the fastest moving, most passionate, violent and dramatic scenes in all opera.

Outside the Bullring at Seville. Act IV, Carmen

There is much more to *Carmen* than the musical highlights described in the summary of the plot. A highly descriptive instrumental *Overture* or *Prelude* played before the curtain rises on Act I, "sets the stage" musically by contrasting the jubilant music of the bullring with the foreboding music that expresses the tragic fate of the lovers. *The Prelude to Act III* summons up the atmosphere of the lonely mountain pass, and another *Prelude to Act IV* is really a lively and agitated Spanish dance and introduces the bullring scene very suitably. There are beautiful choruses including the children's chorus and the chorus of cigarette girls in Act I, background choruses in Act II, especially in the *Toreador Song*, the opening *Smuggler's Chorus* in Act III, and *Escamillo's Entry* in Act IV. The wild gypsy

49

dancing at the beginning of Act II provides a wonderful opportunity for a ballet. Four different settings along with military uniforms, colorful gypsy dresses and the elaborate toreador outfits assure a varied and always interesting stage picture.

After you have become familiar with some of the arias (an operatic word for songs) and know and understand the plot, you may want to listen to the entire opera. Between the arias, duets, trios, etc. there is sung dialogue (recitative). In *Carmen*, Bizet had actually used spoken dialogue, but later this was set to music by a colleague of the composer. (Bizet died thinking *Carmen* was not a success, perhaps because of the spoken dialogue.) Of course, the final step is to try to get to see a live performance by a good company.

What we have done with *Carmen* can be done with any opera. If you are attracted to a particular aria or selection you may hear on radio, T.V. or at a concert, get a "highlight" or "selections" record for the opera in question. Read a plot summary (there are any number of books of opera stories, many with descriptions and analyses of the highlights) or get the opera *libretto* (book), which usually contains a line by line translation into English. When you've become familiar with a few of the arias and know how they fit into the plot, then try the complete opera.

As you listen, remember the points we considered in previous chapters. *Micaela's Aria* in *Carmen* is a perfect example of a three part form ABA. *The Gypsy Dance* is an example of the cumulative *crescendo* we described in the section on dynamics in Chapter II as it builds, not only in volume, but in speed and tension. A great singer performing the role of Carmen should offer a study in vocal tone color as she is alternately seductive, haughty, cruel, mocking, reckless and so on. The use of rhythms and instruments to create the Spanish feeling is worth studying. How well does Bizet suit the music to the stage action? The more you listen and analyze, the more you will hear and enjoy.

There are, of course, operas in which there are few if any "highlights" (arias or set ensemble numbers). These are works where the orchestra and voices are given equal importance and are blended into a unified texture instead of the voices being dominant and the orchestra supportive. They require more experience and a more discerning ear to appreciate fully, but they, too, can be very much enjoyed. They are usually slower moving, more philosophic and generally more involved than the so-called "popular" operas. Since so much of their substance is allotted to the orchestra, the listener must not only be familiar with plot and meanings as expressed in words, but also with the more abstract musical material and ideas being worked over in the orchestra in what is referred to as symphonic style. Most of the operas by Wagner and many modern operas fall into this category.

Some other forms of musical theatre have developed along with opera. Most important of these is the ballet, where everything is danced or pantomimed instead of being sung. The well known ballets are based on fairy tales such as *The Sleeping Beauty* or *Cinderella*, which is not surprising since the world of ballet is even more unreal than the world of opera. But some ballets deal with more adult theatre and *Romeo and Juliet* and *Carmen* have been staged entirely in dance. Again costumes, scenery, and the constantly changing movements and formations of the dancers are fascinating to watch when coupled with the many musical masterpieces that have been composed for the ballet. This combination of movement and music is so interesting in and of itself that many ballets have no plot at all and simply present us with abstract dance patterns. Ballet prospered most significantly in Russia where Tchaikovsky, Stravinsky and Prokofiev all contributed important works to be danced. But choreographers (those who create the dance steps and patterns) often borrow music that was never intended for dance or stage and create ballets around it. Thus Debussy's lovely pastoral *Prelude to the Afternoon of a Faun* and Copland's completely abstract *Concerto for Clarinet* are part of the ballet repertoire. Frequently the choreographer is a fine musician and he creates dance patterns that outline and even clarify the complexities of the music, as when two dancers represent two melodies in counterpoint and the eye helps the ear to differentiate them.

Operetta or light opera is generally comic, tuneful in an almost "pop" style and employs spoken dialogue between musical numbers.

Offenbach, Johann Strauss, Gilbert and Sullivan, Victor Herbert, Franz Lehar and others wrote operettas. Later this type of show became the musical comedy and still later the Broadway musical, the evolution seeming to change the balance between plot and music. Whereas the early operettas and musical comedies used generally silly plots as an excuse for songs and choruses, the later musical gave more importance to the plot and tried to integrate the songs—as in *My Fair Lady* based on *Pygmalion* by George Bernard Shaw. An exception to this are the operettas of Gilbert and Sullivan where, although the plots are nonsensical, Gilbert's very sophisticated and highly satirical lyrics are just as important as Sullivan's music.

Finally we must consider words and music as they occur in religion. In the early history of music, the prime force in its development was the church. Even for primitive men, ritual, prayer and music were all tied together much as they are today. Church music now ranges from ancient Hebraic and Gregorian chants, still used, through simple and traditional hymns to elaborate cantatas for full chorus, organ, orchestra and soloists. The largest of these works are called oratorios because they derived from the attempt to reinforce with music the Bible lessons, given in the oratory (chapel). They are very like opera except that they are set to religious texts and are performed without costumes, scenery or action. To make up for this lack, a part is usually included for a narrator who sings in recitative and keeps the story going, but there are arias and choruses and orchestral interludes. Many great composers have written oratorios. Handel's *Messiah* with its famous *Hallelujah Chorus* is probably best known, but Mendelssohn's *Elijah*, Haydn's *Creation*, Bach's *St. Matthew Passion* are other examples. They may be approached in exactly the same way as opera.

An understanding of the types of voices encountered in opera and on the concert stage will increase listening pleasure. Voices are classified by range and quality.

The female voices are:
soprano (high)

coloratura—the highest and most agile voice, able to execute very florid and rapid passages.

lyric—less showy and generally warmer voice than the coloratura.

dramatic—heavier and more powerful than the coloratura or lyric soprano. (Some sopranos are capable of singing in more than one of the above categories or styles.)

mezzo-soprano—lower in range than the sopranos.

contralto (or alto)—the lowest female voice. (The unchanged voice of the young boy can also be classified as soprano or alto.)

The male voices are:

tenor (high)

lyric—smooth, warm, easily produced, like the lyric soprano.

dramatic—heavier and more powerful than the lyric tenor, required for the Wagner operas, among others.

counter-tenor—higher than the tenor and rather rare, having a *falsetto* quality (like a man imitating a woman's voice very skillfully, but retaining a masculine character); used mostly in early and Baroque music.

baritone—lower than the tenor. (The large majority of adult males have baritone voices.)

bass-baritone—slightly lower and heavier in quality than the baritone.

bass—the lowest male voice.

Opera and oratorio call for a variety of voices. *Carmen* requires a mezzo-soprano or contralto for the title role, a lyric tenor for Don José, a lyric soprano for Micaela, and a baritone for Escamillo.

VIII

PROGRAM MUSIC

It is no great trick for a composer to communicate very specific ideas with words and the human voice. But music can be made to describe things and to tell stories entirely without the voice and with only the merest hint of literary help. We call descriptive or narrative music program music, because it follows a program—that is, it is bound to deal with whatever it wants to describe or to follow the sequence of events in the story it wants to tell.

Some kinds of description have become almost standard. Bird calls, thunder, storms, the sea both calm and turbulent, winds from breezes to cyclones, a peaceful countryside, the animal noises of a farmyard or a jungle, brooks and rivers—all these, and many more manifestations of nature are easily imitated in the orchestra or on the piano or other instruments. We can find ourselves whisked from Spain to Hong Kong and then to New York City or Paris in the short time we spend listening to a few records or a single concert. Even the hustle and rush of urban life, the noise and force of heavy industry, the athletic field, railroads—all have been successfully evoked by clever composers. As we mentioned in Chapter I, the whole business of war and battle and glory and patriotism, as well as the grim and tragic aspects of man's inhumanity to man is music's province.

Only rarely does the composer resort to literal quoting of descriptive sounds. Tchaikovsky did call for a real cannon to be fired in the finale of the *1812 Overture*. Respighi introduces an actual recording of a nightingale's song or call in his *Pines of Rome* and Gershwin calls for authentic French taxi horns in *An American in Paris*. But this is the easy way out. Composers prefer to describe less realistically, using the power of suggestion instead. The rural countryside is peacefully sunny, its quiet broken only by the small sounds of birds and insects, so the composer seeks to create a quiet, sunny mood. If he succeeds, the responsive listener may feel and recognize the quiet of the country. However, if he has not been informed of the composer's intention through a title or an explanatory program note, the listener may experience a quiet mood not at all related to the countryside.

Let us examine a specific piece. Debussy's *Prelude to the Afternoon of a Faun* to which we made passing reference earlier, was inspired by a poem of Mallarmé. Briefly it tells of a young faun, that

Afternoon of a Faun in Ancient Greece.

mythological half goat, half human creature of which the god, Pan, was the adult embodiment. The faun awakens in a forest glade alongside a stream where streaks of sun break through the trees and warm him. Has he dreamt of beautiful nymphs and playful frolics and passionate embraces or has he really experienced these visions? The images grow more vague and the sun warmer. Perhaps if he sleeps again he will recapture the dream—or the reality. He dozes off. Debussy has given us a tone poem that vividly summons up not only the forest setting and the sensuous and amorous imaginings of the young faun but even the feeling of antiquity, so that the listener is carried back to ancient Greece where fauns lived in forests. So effective is this orchestral piece that it has been made into a ballet

Afternoon of a Faun in modern setting of a dance studio.

several times. The first version was danced by the legendary Nijinsky and was faithful to Mallarmé's poem with a setting in an ancient Greek forest. But more recently, the New York City Ballet has staged it so that it takes place in a modern dance studio where a young male dancer, exhausted by excessive practicing, lies asleep on the floor in the middle of the studio. A girl dancer enters and begins to work out slowly. He becomes aware of her and they dance together. They become more intensely involved with each other but she leaves and he sinks back into exhausted sleep. Did he dream their meeting?

In this version there is no forest or stream, no fauns or nymphs. There is only the stark and empty dance studio and a boy and a girl. And yet the quiet pastoral mood of the music works, as does its passionate climax. Debussy loved to evoke musical pictures of nature and did it as successfully as any composer ever did. But, if the listener is guided into thinking only in terms of a kind of love-dream episode in bare modern surroundings, the music fits just as well.

When music attempts storytelling it is more definitely pinpointed, but then it also depends more heavily on explanatory notes. *The Sorcerer's Apprentice* by Paul Dukas tells of a magician's assistant who, when his master leaves, attempts to try his hand at magic. He casts a spell on a broom and orders it to fetch him water, and since he utters the proper incantation, the broom obeys. But as pail after pail is dumped at his feet and the water level begins to rise, the apprentice finds he has forgotten the words to stop the broom. Desperately, he tries to destroy it by breaking it in half only to find each half bringing water causing the place to flood twice as fast. His panic increases until, just as he is about to drown, the magician appears, works his magic so that the waters recede, and then vanishes.

Dukas starts with eerie, magical, atmospheric music which leads into the equally mysterious but more assertive uttering of the magic words (muted trumpets). A few nervous twitchings in a low register signal the first stirrings of the broomstick and these soon develop into a fairly steady galloping rhythm. The composer even works in a kind of wave or rising tide effect as the water keeps coming and the assistant tries vainly to stop it. The breaking of the broom and the resumption of the water works is clearly marked, and the excitement and agitation that follows is even greater than before. The climax is reached with the return of the magician.

The question arises as to just how well the music tells the story. To test this, *The Sorcerer's Apprentice* was played to a class, none of whom had ever heard it before. No hint of its subject matter or even of its title was given, but each member of the class was asked to write the story he thought the music was supposed to tell. No two stories were alike and none was like the one the composer had in mind. However, many members of the class had caught the mysterious and "spooky" quality of the magic sections and had built that feeling into their stories. Almost all had sensed the rising excitement and the feeling of impending danger or disaster, but only a few related the danger to flooding or water. Some found the rhythm descriptive of horses or other animals, but one described witches hobbling around on broomsticks. Apparently the general atmosphere and background of the story is readily discernible or audible in the music, but for specific plot details the listener needs the program note. It is for this reason that Rimsky-Korsakov in his very popular suite, *Scheherezade*, shies away from specific stories, but supplies the listener with, in his own words, "hints to direct but slightly the hearer's fancy on the path which my own fancy had traveled, and to leave more minute and particular conceptions to the will and mood of each listener."

Scheherezade is based on the *Arabian Nights* wherein a Sultan, convinced by a fickle first wife that all women are faithless, puts each succeeding wife to death after one night of marriage. Scheherezade, not only beautiful but clever, delays her execution by telling the Sultan stories too long to finish in one night and starting a new one before bedtime the next night. Her skill is so great and her husband's curiosity so insatiable that the trick works for a thousand and one nights by which time the Sultan is hopelessly in love with her and her life is spared. The composer represents the Sultan with a stern, powerful, and rather somber theme in the full orchestra and Scheherezade with a graceful, very Oriental tune for solo violin with harp accompaniment (perhaps reminiscent of the ancient minstrels who sang with harp accompaniment). These two themes appear from time to time in the four sections of the work, but that is as specific as the composer ever gets. For the rest, he gives us vague titles and lets the music in all its splendid Oriental color work its way with our imaginations. The first movement is called *The Sea and the Vessel of Sinbad* and we hear the sea in long gentle swells and huge crashing waves, and we sense the endless distance to the unbroken horizon, and we know that Sinbad sailed such a sea. But no incidents or adventures are described. They are left for us to supply. The second movement is called *The Tale of the Prince Kalender.* A Kalender is a wandering beggar or fakir and many such wanderers tell many tales in the Arabian Nights. Rimsky-Korsakov gives us no indication as to what story he had in mind, but we can certainly hear that it has a quietly thoughtful beginning, that it works up to a frenzied celebration or dance, that this is interrupted by military fanfares and wild dashes, perhaps of horses. In the third movement, *The Young Prince and the Young Princess* the mood turns romantic—a love song, perhaps in a garden with gently swaying palms—then an exotic Oriental dance and a return of the love song with surges of great passion, but no detailed story. The last movement has a three part title—*Festival at Bagdad. The Sea. The Ship Goes to Pieces on a Rock.* The music follows this scenario and is at first a crowded, excited, colorful Oriental festival which gives way to the sea of the first movement, but now a wild and raging sea, a sea which must inevitably wreck the ship. In the quiet which follows the storm we hear a much tamed Sultan and a lovely Scheherezade no longer in fear of her life.

Some composers feel, however, that music can detail very specific ideas and actions, and, with the help of sufficient explanation, it frequently does. There is no question that music speaks a language of emotion and that these emotions can be focused into channels dictated by the composer. But each of us brings his own unique reactions to music and if the composer is too rigid and confining in his concept he will destroy or inhibit our enjoyment, by limiting our personal involvement.

It is essential that program music be good music in its own right. Clever effects cannot make up for poor melodies, dull harmony, or inadequate development of musical ideas. One should be able to listen to program music with no prior knowledge of its subject matter and still find it a satisfying musical experience.

Program music has been with us from the very beginning. It became very popular in the middle of the nineteenth century when the orchestra came into fuller development so that its descriptive possibilities could be exploited by such composers as Franz Liszt. He is credited with having created the tone poem (a long descriptive or narrative composition for orchestra) of which the three works analyzed in this chapter are good examples. But long before Liszt, Beethoven had written his *Pastoral Symphony* (#6) in which he describes a day in the country. Berlioz also wrote much program music. And much descriptive music has been composed for solo instruments, especially the piano, where titles like *The Cuckoo, Papillons (Butterflies), The Bee, Rush Hour in Hong Kong* abound.

IX

JUST MUSIC
ABSOLUTE MUSIC
FORM

We have seen how music can describe, communicate, picture and narrate with some help from the written word, the voice, and the arts of the theatre. We will now turn to music which refuses all such help—music which presents itself to us entirely in terms of music—no story, no pictures, no words—just tone, rhythm, harmony, melody and dynamics. We call such music pure or absolute music. It makes its appeal entirely through the beauty of its melodies and the variety of moods they can inspire in us; through its harmonies and the emotional reactions they can generate; through its rhythms and the physical impulses they can excite—all these skillfully seasoned with appropriate dashes of tone color and dynamics. It does us little good to ask, therefore, what Mozart's *Symphony in G Minor* is about unless we are willing to look for the answer in the music itself. Then we discover that it is a fairly long work in four separate movements, each movement in a different tempo or speed, and each creating a different mood or series of moods. We note, too, that the overall impression we get from listening is one of grace and precision so characteristic of all of Mozart's music. The movements differ not only in tempo, but in their forms or patterns of internal structure. Since the work is longer than the song forms we examined in Chapter VI, these patterns are expansions of those small AB and ABA forms. Long works, however, generally contain several different melodic, rhythmic and harmonic ideas and these very often are themselves small forms. So we get a kind of architectural pyramid beginning with a theme (melody) which may or may not be a small form but which, along with other themes, is part of a movement

61

which is an expanded form. This movement, in turn, is part of a longer work in several movements which are organized to provide variety and contrast in all the musical elements.

How does the composer expand a form? Bearing in mind that recognition is one of the great pleasures of listening, he limits himself to two or three themes in a given movement. To have more would make recognition difficult and listening too confusing. Between these themes he provides bridge or transitional material which frequently is created out of bits and pieces (sometimes called motives or fragments) of the theme just stated. The theme has a recognizable character and set dimensions. It may be a repeated phrase (AA or a two part or three part form (AB or ABA) or in another pattern. The transition will have a less stable, more restless feeling as if it were moving on and leading into something else, which is exactly what it is doing, usually taking us to a new theme in a new key.

After the themes have been stated, the composer may wish to develop them. He may change the rhythm and the harmonies, use all or fragments of them in melodic sequence (see Chapter II), combine one with another in counterpoint, invert them, change the instrumentation and in a thousand ways elaborate on them so as to build to a climax. This development section (or working out of thematic material) is limited only by his ingenuity and good taste.

To find his way through a development the listener must be very familiar with the themes so that he can recognize them when changed or fragmented. But should the listener lose his way, the composer usually considerately refreshes his memory after the development by bringing back the themes pretty much in their original form in what is called a restatement or recapitulation.

While melody provides the easiest guideposts for the untrained ear, it is not the only musical element that determines form. Harmony is also very important. First themes are stated in the tonic or home key, and second themes in a different key, usually the dominant (the key most closely related to the tonic and built on the fifth note of the tonic scale), but sometimes the relative or parallel minor or major key. Development sections are generally a kaleidoscope of constantly changing keys; that is, they are highly modulatory which imparts interest and excitement. In the recapitulation, the return to the tonic key for both themes not only reinforces their recognition, but reestablishes stability and balance in a sort of harmonic ABA.

The form just described is referred to as *sonata–allegro* form. It can be further expanded by the addition of introductory and closing or summary material (coda). It is perhaps easier to understand in diagram.

Sonata–Allegro Form

    Introduction (optional, and, when used, usually slow)

A. Exposition or Statement

    Theme I—tonic key

        transition

    Theme II—dominant key

        transition

    Coda (ending)—sometimes Theme III (Closing Theme)
      —dominant key. The Coda is usually based on material from Themes I and II.

B. Development—modulatory elaboration or working out of material from Exposition. This section can be quite extensive. However, if very short or reduced to a mere transition, the work becomes a sonatina (little sonata).

A. Recapitulation or Restatement

    Theme I—tonic key

        transition

    Theme II—tonic key

        transition

    Coda—sometimes Theme III (Closing theme)—tonic key; usually more extensive than when it appears in the Exposition, since here it must finish off the whole movement.

The expansion of the three part form is evident in the sequence of Exposition (Statement)—Development—Recapitulation (Restatement)—a large ABA.

Extremely important in eighteenth and nineteenth century music, sonata–allegro form is fundamental to the symphony, the concerto, the concert overture, the solo sonata, and most chamber music as we shall see in subsequent chapters.

Another expanded form is the theme and variations. Here, only one theme is used, usually a small two or three part form. It is then treated to a series of variations much in the manner of development, but with less tendency to break up the theme into fragments.

The rondo is a long form that keeps returning to its main theme, but introduces other themes in between. It usually uses transitional material between themes. The two most frequent rondos are:

The Five Part Rondo
ABAB (or C) A
The Seven Part Rondo
ABACABA

A coda may be added at the end, and each section may be a small form. When C in the seven part rondo is a development of previous material (rather than new material), it becomes pretty hard to tell the rondo from sonata-allegro form.

The minuet is really two small forms put together. It consists of ABA in which A is repeated and then BA is repeated. A second section, called the trio, follows consisting of CDC in which C is repeated and then DC is repeated. Finally, the original ABA returns, this time without repeats.

Minuet: A(repeated) BA(repeated)
Trio: C(repeated) DC(repeated)
Minuet: ABA (no repeats)

This, then, is a large three part form made up of two small ones. The scherzo, introduced in the nineteenth century, is the same form changed in style from the dignified minuet to a more playful mood.

Some large works of pure music place less emphasis on strict form. These are called fantasy, rhapsody, ballade etc. While they don't fit any of the patterns described, they are not formless. Rather they are in free form, with patterns of their own. They do repeat themes and develop them. They provide the listener with opportunities for pleasurable recognition.

Many small forms are used in absolute music. Nocturnes, preludes, etudes and many kinds of dances such as gavottes, mazurkas, waltzes are among these. Many composers have specialized in small forms, among them Chopin, Johann Strauss Jr., the waltz king, and John Philip Sousa, the march king.

There is, however, one fascinating small form we should look at more closely. The fugue is a contrapuntal form and was used long before sonata-allegro form was even thought of. It consists of a series of interweaving melodic lines called voices whether sung or played on instruments. It is something like a round since each voice starts out with the same subject or tune. Unlike the round, however, the voices are not all introduced at the same pitch. And once the second voice is introduced the first one does not slavishly repeat the subject as in a round, but instead weaves new melodic material around it. The fugue can be written for any reasonable number of voices, usually three, four or five. The more voices, the more intricate the counterpoint. When the subject has been introduced in all the voices, one after the other, the exposition or statement of the fugue is complete. There follows a development section, not unlike that of the sonata, where the subject can be inverted, fragmented, expanded or contracted in rhythm, introduced in overlapping entrances, one voice entering with the subject before the previous voice has finished with it (*stretto*), and where excitement and tension build up until finally the subject returns for the last time, complete and in its original form presented so as to dominate the ending—in effect a recapitulation or restatement. So again we have an ABA form. Though brought to its highest development by Bach in the early eighteenth century, the fugue has continued to challenge composers even today. Even when they do not write complete fugues many composers use fugal techniques in compositions that are otherwise not very contrapuntal.

Bach wrote most of his fugues for organ or clavichord (an early form of piano), but many of these have been transcribed for orchestra, and should you want to listen to one, try the *Little Fugue in G Minor* in such a transcription. It is a bit easier to follow when the voices are presented in different instruments than when everything is played on one instrument. The subject here is easily recognized and remembered, the work is quite short, and every facet of fugal writing described above is clearly audible in it. The catchy tune of this four voice fugue builds with amazing energy and drive to a climax of great power and dignity in a very few minutes and provides a most satisyfing listening experience.

We started this chapter on absolute music by emphasizing its total use of purely musical elements and then dealt at some length with form or musical design as determined by melody and harmony. Since we have already dealt with the elements in Chapter II, we expect the reader is developing an awareness of them, and is listening more perceptively and more "participantly" all the time.

He therefore should begin to notice that rhythm is also a fundamental part of form. The alternation of fast and slow movements in long works provides variety and contrast. And within each movement frequent significant rhythmic contrast between themes serves the same function on a smaller scale. Variations in dynamics and in instrumentation (tone color) frequently serve to delineate form as well. And all of these enrich the development section.

There is a way of pinning one's listening down a little more precisely with respect to these elements. Without letting your imagination turn too pictorial, you can sit and listen with a pencil and pad, and jot down words or short phrases that describe your reaction to or feeling for the music, section by section, as it goes. Here are some words jotted down by a class hearing the opening melody of the Mozart *G Minor Symphony* for the first time. Note that some students not only wrote the descriptive word or phrase, but added in parenthesis the particular musical element to which they were reacting.

>   running (rhythm)
>   whistling tune (melody)
>   singing violins (melody and tone color)

restless mood
minor key (harmony)
graceful
quiet (dynamics)

It really doesn't matter whether any great agreement exists among the members of a class or group with respect to these words. For instance, "restless mood" and "quiet" might seem contradictory. But if this is the reaction of the person listening and writing the word, and if it helps him to remember the music, this is most important. It so happens that the accompaniment figure in the lower strings is "restless" and the opening dynamic level is "quiet," and thus two students were reacting to two different aspects of the music.

As you become accustomed to using this technique, you will find you are developing a larger vocabulary of words dealing with mood, emotion, movement, color, etc. Try to avoid stringing words together so they begin to build a picture or a story. That would run contrary to the composer's intention where pure music is involved. Rather use these words as recognition and memory aids. Sometimes you will find that the same melody described as "gentle" at one point in the music may have to be described as "powerful" at another point. It is in just this way that the jotting method keeps your listening focused on what the music is saying in musical terms.

We have said little about style in music, largely because this is an element in both program and absolute music, and because we think it can be better treated when we deal with the various historical periods in music. However, the jotting method is also helpful in developing an awareness of stylistic factors, since many of the words you employ will cover more than one facet of the music. Such a word is "graceful" which applies not only to the lovely melody that opens the symphony, but, as we have said, to most of Mozart's music.

X

THE SYMPHONY

No one is quite sure how the symphony got its name. As instrumental music began to develop, especially as a result of the need for more complete and expressive accompaniments for the early operas and oratorios, composers attached the title *Sinfonia* to purely orchestral passages used as introductions or interludes. The word comes from the Greek and means "sounding together"—but why only instrumental music and not vocal? It was used interchangeably with other words such as *Overture* and *Ritornello* and all these words soon came to be applied to instrumental works not necessarily incidental to vocal music.

The idea of separate movements arose from the practice of grouping a series of dance forms together so that slow and fast dances alternated. Such a grouping was called *Overture* or *Sinfonia*, and later *Suite*, the name we use today. While the music was written in the style, rhythm and form of the popular dances of the period, when presented as an *Overture, Sinfonia* or *Suite*, it was generally too intricate and elaborate to dance to and was intended for concert performance or after-dinner entertainment in the homes of the nobility.

The emergence of sonata-allegro form as characteristic of the symphony resulted from a number of influences. Composers were experimenting with new harmonic ideas, supporting more lyric melodies with chordal background rather than treating them contrapuntally. They were, however, reluctant to abandon the challenge of the development section which they carried over from the fugue (and other contrapuntal forms), adapting it to the newer harmonic (homophonic) treatment.

The three part pattern of exposition (statement), development and recapitulation (restatement) was an outgrowth of the dance forms and song forms, the fugue and the composer's instinctive understanding of the importance of repetition and recognition.

By the time we reach the Classical masters, Haydn and Mozart, symphonic form is pretty much set, though in the hands of these two giants it takes on a remarkable clarity and perfection.

Mozart's *Symphony No. 40 in G Minor* is a masterpiece and a model of the form, and we propose now to analyze it in some detail. It is hoped that the reader will follow the analysis while listening to a good recording of the symphony, and that he will feel encouraged to replay passages until he can hear and identify the passage referred to in the analysis. Without hearing the music, what follows will be impossible to understand. For those who can read music we have included thematic examples which can aid in focusing one's listening. But we hope the text is sufficiently clear so that a careful listener won't need them.

The first movement in a fairly rapid tempo has no introduction, but gets directly to the point with the lovely and graceful minor key melody we referred to in the last chapter, played by the string section. This is based on a three note motive repeated three times and rising in a delicate lift. Then, after a breath, the melody descends on the three note motive. The whole pattern is repeated in sequence a tone lower and this comprises the A part of the opening or first theme. The three note motive is then expanded into a broader rhythm, winds are added, a more assertive dynamic level is reached with some spirited chords and we've had the B part of the first theme. The delicate first idea (A) returns, this time with woodwinds above the strings, the repeating sequence a tone higher instead of lower, and leads dirctly into transitional material of a more forceful nature scored for the full orchestra, culminating in a full cadence (stop) in a new key. Thus theme I turns out to be a three part form (ABA). (see Theme I)

Theme II in a major key also begins in the strings with a descending scale figure imitated immediately in the woodwinds and then continued in the strings. This is repeated, reversing the order with woodwinds preceding strings and quickly turns into a transition. Theme II, therefore, consists of just one part, A, repeated. (see Theme II)

The transition leads us to a coda based on fragments (the three

69

note motive) of theme I. These are tossed back and forth between strings and various woodwinds and then blossom into a slightly more complete but modified form of theme I. The exposition or statement ends vigorously. (Your recording may or may not repeat the entire exposition, since many modern conductors consider this repeat optional, but in Mozart's day it was always repeated.)

The development section starts with two chords and a woodwind bridge and then picks up theme IA complete in the violins and takes it through three different keys. Now the lower strings enter with the theme in alternation with the violins. The theme is then reduced to only the descending half and then further reduced to the three note motive, now alternating between strings and woodwinds, continually changing keys and dynamic level. A gentle woodwind bridge built entirely on the three note motive leads us back to the recapitulation (restatement) as theme I almost sneaks back in its original form in the strings, but with an added bassoon. Things proceed much as they did in the exposition except that the transition is much expanded and works its way aound to theme II in the same key as theme I (G minor) instead of in B flat major as in the exposition. Theme II in minor porvides an interesting new effect, but is otherwise treated as before. The coda is also extended with the addition of an imitative passage based on theme IA where second violin is followed by first violin and then by viola all entering with the same melody but in different keys. A vigorous ending brings the movement to a close. In diagram form we can chart this movement as follows:

A. Exposition
    Theme I(ABA) in G minor
        transition
    Theme II(AA) in B flat major (relative major key)
        transition
    Coda based on theme I(A) motive (repeat of Exposition
        optional)

B. Development: Theme I(A) in violins, three ⎤
    times in descending sequence.   ⎥
      Theme I(A) alternating between lower ⎥
      and upper strings, two times.   ⎥
      2nd half of Theme I(A) in descending ⎥   many keys
      sequence three times   ⎰ (modulatory)
      Just the motive in larger, then smaller ⎥
      fragments—woodwinds and strings, fi- ⎥
      nally forming woodwind bridge lead- ⎥
      ing to   ⎦

A. Recapitulation
> Theme I(ABA) in strings with bassoon—then continuing
> > as before in Exposition in G minor
> > transition (extended)
> Theme II(AA) (now in G minor)
> > transition
> Coda based on Theme I(A) motive and extended to in-
> > clude imitative entrances of 1st half of I(A) in upper
> > strings.

The second movement in a contrasting major key (E flat) is a moderately slow movement based on two very simple ideas. The first consists of an upward melodic lift to a series of repeated notes in perfectly even rhythm and the second consists of a series of decorative little two note skips. Mozart opens the movement with the violas on the repeated note idea and adds second violins and first violins in succession on different repeated notes, thus creating harmonic interest. He rounds this off with an adroit melodic twist while the horns pick up the repeated note idea. Two gentle sighs in the violins and two of the little skips are next, and we have the first complete unit of the movement. While built up in seeming piecemeal fashion, these eight measures have a fascinating melodic interest.

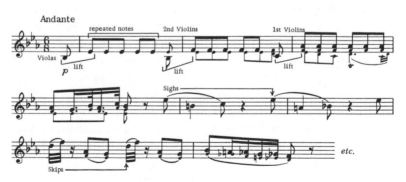

Mozart then repeats the same ideas but this time giving them to the lower strings and using the violins to decorate them with subtle but highly melodic touches. So far we have had AA. Now comes a new combination of these ideas, introducing some dynamic contrast with loud chords interrupting the general quiet and with more importance being given the skip figure and this constitutes B.

A returns shortened and now decorated with woodwinds on the skip motive, but the repeated note emerges in three strong measures of *forte* (loud). Mozart adds a graceful new idea as a sort of closing theme, but with hints of both of the other motives in the background.

The score calls for a repeat of this entire section, but again some recordings omit the repeat.

This first half of the second movement is, therefore, a small form, AABA, with a postlude or closing added. We hesitate to use the word coda, which also means ending, because codas usually don't introduce new material, but work with ideas that have appeared before. In this case the new material is really derived from ideas previously introduced and certainly the old ideas themselves appear so we could call it a coda with some justification.

Mozart expands this small form by going into a short development of the two figures giving the woodwinds the repeated notes while the strings play the skip and then switching the parts. In short order, A reappears exactly as at the beginning of the movement. However, the repetition of A is shortened, B is reintroduced, but not completely, and A returns with its second half first (the gentle sighs this time in the cellos and basses). The first half comes next with modifications and building in force. The closing or coda is then repeated in the proper closing key.

AABA coda—E flat major
Development—modulatory
ABA coda—E flat major

The third movement is a minuet and follows the traditional form to the letter. It opens vigorously in G minor with full orchestra and repeats this section (A). It brightens in B flat, the relative major key (B), returning to the minor in a more complicated treatment (A) and then repeats B and A.

The trio is orchestrated much more lightly and is in G, the parallel major key. Its first part, C, is scored for violins and woodwinds and is repeated. D is scored for low strings and woodwinds and C returns with violins under a lovely duet for French horns, and D and C are repeated.

The minuet is then played again, this time without repeats (ABA). In diagram form:

> Minuet: A (repeated) BA (repeated)
> Trio: C (repeated) DC (repeated)
> Minuet: ABA (no repeats)

The finale or last movement is in sonata-allegro form and begins its exposition with a fast and energetic theme I in G minor that runs through an A (repeated) BA (repeated) pattern, almost too rapidly for the listener to catch it. Here B is only half the length of A and only the second half of A returns so BA together just balance the complete A.

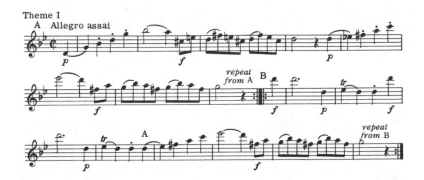

The transition which follows is really built upon fragments of theme I almost in the style of a development as it races headlong and at some length to a brief pause for breath. Theme II seems slower because it is calmer and more lyrical, but the fundamental tempo of the movement remains the same. It unwinds its long melodic line in B flat, the relative major key, first in the strings and then in the winds and so is just A repeated.

It flows into a coda very similar to the transition that preceded it. This exposition, because its speed makes it seem short, is usually repeated in recordings.

The development begins with the whole orchestra in unison announcing theme IA. After tossing it back and forth from one instrument to another for a bit, Mozart begins a contrapuntal treatment of it, a sort of fughetta (little fugue) in stretto (overlapping entrances). This gives way to an antiphonal section with the full winds pitted against the lower strings and alternating on theme IA. The violins enter the alternation which carries through to a pause. Again, the development runs through many keys.

The recapitulation brings back theme I in its original state but without repeats and follows through with much the same transition. Theme II, however, returns in the tonic minor key (note the similarity to the handling of theme II in the first movement). The coda here is a little longer than in the exposition. In diagram form:

A. Exposition:
> Theme I(A) (repeat) (BA) (repeat)—in G minor
> > transition
>
> Theme II(AA) (in relative major key)
> Coda (fragments of Theme I) (exposition usually repeated)

B. Development:
> Theme I(A) in unison, then tossed back and forth, then treated contrapuntally and finally in alternate sections, in many keys.

A. Recapitulation:
> Theme I(ABA)—tonic key
> > transition
>
> Theme II(AA) (in tonic minor key)
> Coda

This, then, is the formal analysis of the *Symphony #40 in G Minor* by Mozart. If you were able to follow it, you should have a better understanding of how a composer works with musical materials in purely musical terms.

If you had difficulty in locating in the music the points described in the analysis, don't hesitate to repeat a passage several times, if necessary, so that you begin to recognize its content. If you have been listening with pencil in hand and jotting down descriptive words or phrases to help you recognize themes or features of the music that stand out or appeal to you, try relating these words to the analysis. For instance, theme I of the first movement we have already described as graceful, but it is also perhaps a little plaintive (or any other adjective you find appropriate). In contrast, theme II is more square cut and cheerful. If you can supply your own descriptive words they will undoubtedly help you more than the words we supply in recognizing themes and sections as they are repeated in the music or as you play them again. Following the formal structure can be fascinating, but your jottings should also serve to remind you that the music speaks to you emotionally. Mozart's symphony has an elegance and precision that speaks of the eighteenth century noble courts for which he wrote. It has a strength and power that reveals much of Mozart, the man, who struggled to free himself from the restrictions of one such court. And it has a warmth and tenderness that tells of his affection for his family and his susceptibility to the charms of the opposite sex. Not only was the symphony carefully worked out as we have seen but we must not forget that it was also deeply felt.

XI

THE CONCERTO
THE CONCERT OVERTURE

The concerto is a symphony with a featured soloist (or soloists) and, like the symphony, has its roots in earlier instrumental forms. In today's large orchestras a huge body of strings serves to balance a large complement of winds, brasses and percussion. The dynamics available range from the merest whisper of a single muted violin to the thunderous massed effect of one hundred players blasting off the roof, and the variations in tone color are infinite. But, earlier, when groups were smaller and mostly strings, the whole expressive dynamic and tone color range was much more limited. Composers, therefore, would contrast a few players against the whole group, or divide the group in two (double orchestra) and use the two groups responsively (antiphonally) sometimes imitating echo effects. These devices produced a form called the concerto grosso, a work in several movements, in which two, three or four instruments formed the solo group, supported by and contrasted with the rest of the string players (seldom more than twenty players all told). Archangelo Corelli wrote beautiful *Concerti Grossi* as did Johann Sebastian Bach (the *Brandenburg Concerti*). As the orchestra grew in size, and, with the addition of new instruments, in flexibility, and as the taste for virtuosity developed, it was inevitable that the concerto would evolve into a show piece for a star performer.

Like the symphony, it is a work in several movements, usually three—a fast first movement generally in sonata-allegro form, a slow second movement and a fast third movement either in rondo or sonata-allegro form. The minuet or scherzo (third movement) of the symphony is dropped, although there are a few concertos with four movements.

79

In the Classical concertos of Haydn, Mozart and Beethoven the exposition of the first movement is given in its entirety first to the orchestra, and it is only in its repeat that the soloist is heard. But in later works the soloist may be heard right at the beginning, or a give and take established between orchestra and soloist.

Again, in the Classical concerto, the orchestra, after its initial statement is usually relegated to the background as an accompaniment to the virtuoso with only an occasional burst of importance in a transition or finale passage. But in the Romantic and Modern periods, composers utilize the full palette of the orchestra, sometimes subordinating the soloist to the orchestra, or simply integrating him into the orchestral texture. Of course, he is still given much opportunity to shine, and, if anything, the technical demands of the later works are greater and more intricate than the early ones.

There are some concertos for multiple instruments; (Mozart— *Concerto in Eb* for two pianos and the *Symphonie Concertante* for violin and viola; Beethoven—*Triple Concerto* for violin, cello and piano; Brahms—*Double Concerto* for violin and cello are among the most well known), but most of the literature is written for solo piano or solo violin with orchestra, with a good number of concertos for the cello and a few for practically every other instrument including even guitar, percussion and organ.

In the early concertos it was customary for the composer to write a long pause for the orchestra in the first movement and sometimes again in the other movements during which the soloist improvised music (theoretically on the spur of the moment) based on the movement's themes. When the composer himself was the soloist, as was frequently the case at the time, this worked out pretty well, and the cadenza, as such an improvised passage was called, could emerge as a very exciting part of the music. But when a brilliant performer who was not talented in composition improvised his own cadenza, it often did not measure up to the standard of the rest of the music. So, in later works it is generally written out by the composer. It still affords the soloist some glorious moments alone in which to display his virtuosity.

Beethoven's *Concerto in D Major* for violin and orchestra is certainly one of the greatest works in this form. The reader can apply the same method of analysis we used with the Mozart symphony in the last chapter. A good recording, careful listening and jottings and a willingness to repeat passages until they are really familiar to you will yield great dividends in enjoyment. This time we will supply only a skeletal outline and leave the details to you to discover.

The first movement, *Allegro ma non troppo* (not too fast) opens with five strokes on the kettle drum. These are really part of theme I and are fundamental to the entire movement.

Exposition:
> Theme I—kettle drum (timpani) beat followed by hymn-like theme in woodwinds and then drum beat figure in the strings—Tonic—D major

> transition ending in first violin bridge passage to
> Theme II—in woodwinds based on scale and songlike in character over strings on drum beat figure—Tonic—D major (see Theme II)
> This is then repeated in D minor (parallel key) by violins with a running accompaniment in lower strings and the drum beat figure softly in the brasses
> transition

81

Theme II
Oboe & Winds

*Theme II repeat-
ed in minor key
in strings*

Closing theme—broad and full—sounding played responsively
between high and low strings—Tonic—D major

Closing theme
Violins

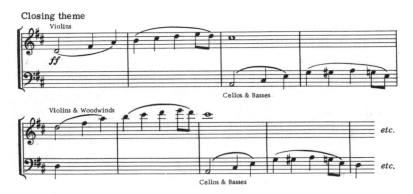

Cellos & Basses

Violins & Woodwinds

etc.

etc.

Cellos & Basses

(This exposition is completely and entirely for the orchestra.)

The violin solo enters now on an introductory cadenza-like passage which leads to exposition repeated with soloist.

Theme I—solo violin and woodwinds—violin part highly elaborated—Tonic—D major
transition (embelished with solos)
Theme II—woodwinds and solo in major; strings and solo
variation in minor—this time in the more usual dominant
key (A major and minor)
transition
Closing theme—this time softly in strings with much technical display work in solo violin (also now in A major) leading to

Development: ⎰Transitional material for full orchestra
all for full ⎱ Theme II major and minor for full orchestra
orchestra   transition
(we call ⎰Closing theme
this *tutti*)   Violin entrance like original entrance but in a
and all in   different key leading to
new keys   Theme I in new key (minor) and developed
(modula-   in fragments with rhythmic variation on
tory)   drum beat figure. Then, with horns on the
five note figure and strings on sustained
chords, the violin solo becomes very beautifully rhapsodic and eventually builds up in
tension and leads into

Recapitulation: Full Orchestra (*tutti*)

Theme I—Tonic—D major
transition (leading to violin entrance, again similar to
original entrance, but continuing on transitional material
for some length)

Theme II—woodwinds and solo in major; strings and solo
variations in minor—Tonic (as in the exposition for orchestra)
transition

Closing Theme—again as at end of second exposition, softly
and with much technical display work in solo violin, but
now in D major leading to the

Coda—transitional material for full orchestra (just like the
beginning of the development) building to a grand pause
for the

Cadenza—(Beethoven did write a cadenza, but showier ones
by some of the great violinists, notably Fritz Kriesler, are
frequently heard.) Since the cadenza elaborates on the
themes of the movement it is very well placed here as part
of the coda. Usually the cadenza ends with the orchestra
entering on one of the principal themes while the soloist
trills or decorates above it. But here Beethoven has the violin solo play the second theme simply and straightforwardly
while the orchestral strings supply the barest *pizzicato* back-

ground, the horns and oboes recalling the drumbeat and the bassoon the closing theme; a final flourish from the violin and a few chords from the full orchestra end the movement.

The second movement is slow (*larghetto*) and is a theme and variations. The theme is announced by the muted strings and has a quiet, reverential, almost prayerlike quality. It is in the key of G, the subdominant, providing harmonic change from the first movement's concentration on tonic and dominant (D and A).

The first two variations are provided by lacy elaboration in the solo violin. The third restates the theme in the strings but adds winds without solo violin and leads into a free intermediate section dominated by the violin. A fourth variation brings back the theme in the strings, *pizzicato* under the continuing delicate filigree of the solo which grows ever more ethereal. A sudden *forte* in the orchestra shatters the spell and a cadenza carries us into the third movement which is a rollicking rondo. It opens with a spirited solo for the violin—a real country fiddle tune in the style of a jig which is immediately repeated two octaves higher in the solo part and then again by the full orchestra. This is the principal subject of the rondo.

A (AAA)—Tonic—D major

transition—violin solo and horns and woodwinds

B short—played responsively by full orchestra and solo violin (double-stops)—Dominant—A major and minor

transition dominated by rapid technical violin solo passages with hints of A in the orchestra leading us back to

A (AAA)—Tonic—D major

transition—very short

C in minor key—a short AABA form as a duet between solo violin and bassoon. C is more lyric than either of the two first ideas—in G minor (subdominant)

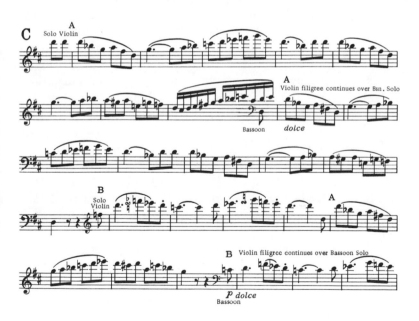

transition

A (ΛΛΛ)—Tonic—D major
transition—violin solo and horns and woodwinds
B short—as above and now in tonic—D major and minor
transition same as transition after B above but in different key leading to
Cadenza—beginning on the dominant, A, and followed by a modulatory
Coda—based mostly on A, beginning with re-entry of low strings under solo violin trills and building to a rousing finish.

Musicians argue whether Beethoven wrote a five part rondo (ABACA with the coda beginning with the second appearance of B, since it is so short, and including the cadenza and coda outlined above) or a seven part rondo (ABACABA with the cadenza and coda counting as the final A). But for the listener such arguments are unimportant. Even discerning the correct form is unimportant as long as one follows and is aware of the ways in which the composer is repeating a theme or fragmenting it or modifying it. If you mistake a transition for a development, no harm is done, since they both feature the same techniques and differ mostly as to how they are placed in the music. It is not critical that your analysis be accurate, but rather that you listen analytically. And with the two works we have so far explored (Mozart and Beethoven) this may be difficult, for both works are so attractive melodically that one is easily lulled into just listening. Again, this is no sin. One should listen to enjoy. But when one listens "participantly" the enjoyment is fuller and richer.

*   *   *

Before we end our discussion of the use of sonata-allegro form in orchestral works (symphony and concerto), we should mention the concert overture. This is a work in a single movement, frequently partly programatic, but generally in sonata-allegro form and often having nothing to do with an opera or theatrical production. Such an overture is Mendelssohn's *Fingal's Cave* inspired by a trip made by the composer to the Hebrides, islands off the coast of Scotland. Brilliantly descriptive of wind, surf, birds and the echo effects of a seaside cave, the overture is nevertheless a fine example of strict sonata-allegro form. Nor does it serve as an introduction or prelude to anything.

Similarly in his overture *Romeo and Juliet*, referred to in an earlier chapter, Tchaikowsky takes the three dramatic elements of Shakespeare's play, represents each with an appropriate theme and then works the whole thing out in sonata-allegro form. We hear first the somber wisdom of Friar Lawrence as theme I, then the agitation of the feud between the Montagues and the Capulets as theme II and finally the deeply passionate love of Romeo and Juliet as a closing theme of the exposition.

Theme I (Friar Lawrence)

Theme II (Feud)

Theme III (Love)

There follows a development in which the feud theme effectively smothers the Friar and the lovers and then a recapitulation in which the love theme becomes poignantly tragic and a coda in which it becomes transcendent and ethereal. Thus the broad outlines of the story are adhered to without sacrificing the form. Many concert overtures could really qualify as tone poems. What sets them apart is the way they work descriptive or narrative ideas into the confines of a purely musical form (the sonata-allegro).

XII

CHAMBER MUSIC—THE SONATA

Artists in every field seek to achieve desired effects with the greatest possible economy of means. The symphony, the opera, the ballet all employ large forces and frequently impress by virtue of their bigness. Sometimes their sheer volume makes music sound better than it really is. Composers, therefore, have always shown great respect for smaller groups of instruments. Working with from two to ten instruments enables them to present their musical ideas with a special clarity, transparency and intimacy. They can, within the more delicate framework, explore moods and emotions less appropriate for large groups. Music composed for such small groups is called chamber music since it can readily be performed in a room instead of a concert hall (although in actual practice today it is very often performed in concert halls). Whereas in a large orchestra whole sections of instruments play the same part so that groups of ten basses, twelve cellos, fourteen violas, sixteen second violins and eighteen first violins will perform each part, in chamber music each player is on his own. Thus, in a string quartet the four musicians play four different parts.

Duets, trios, quartets, quintets, etc., for strings or strings and piano, or for strings with other instruments, or for woodwinds—for any instrumental combination even including the harmonica—make up the chamber music literature. But by far the most important chamber music form is the string quartet with the string trio and the string quintet runners up.

The string quartet consists of first and second violin, viola and cello. The piano quartet drops one of the violins and adds a piano. The trio uses a violin, cello and piano and the quintet adds a piano, or an extra cello, or an extra viola, or a clarinet or almost any other instrument to the instruments of the string quartet.

89

Chamber music grew out of the same roots as the orchestral forms. The *concerto grosso*, especially, in its use of a small group of solo instruments contrasted with the larger orchestra, pointed the way. Chamber works are usually in four movements in the same sequence as the classical symphony with a first movement in sonata-allegro form, a slow movement (small form or theme and variations) a minuet or scherzo, and a finale (a rondo or again a sonata-allegro).

Because the instrumental resources are limited, composers are challenged to create interest and excitement in other ways. Melodic lines are tossed back and forth among the instruments and many contrapuntal techniques such as imitation and fugue abound. With the small number of instruments, it is relatively easy to hear this give and take and the instrumental interweaving becomes fascinating in its own right. While the scale of effects is less than orchestral it is nonetheless amazingly varied, and ranges from the expected calm and quiet of a small group to rather surprising climaxes of tensions and tempests. The quartets (and other chamber music) of the later Romantic, Impressionist and early Modern composers are especially interesting with respect to instrumental effects, and the Ravel and Debussy quartets astound us with the multiplicity of exciting and beautiful sounds they create.

Since the same method of analysis we applied to the symphony and the concerto is appropriate for chamber music, and since the forms are much the same, we will not analyze any specific chamber work. We suggest that the listener pursue such an analysis himself, starting, perhaps, with the first quartet by Beethoven (Opus 18, #1) or the Mozart *Clarinet Quintet* (K. 581). We suggest these because their themes are easily differentiated, but almost any Haydn, Mozart, Beethoven or Schubert chamber work will do as well.

We come now to the solo sonata, an extended form in three or four movements following the same patterns as the symphony, concerto or chamber work, but for solo instrument, or solo instrument and piano. The name sonata derives from the Latin *sonare*—to sound —presumably on an instrument. Thus it was distinct from the cantata (*cantare*—to sing). The earliest sonatas were of two types: the *sonata da chiesa* (church sonata) dignified and largely contrapuntal, and the *sonata da camera* (chamber sonata) a collection of dance tunes. So we see the same elements that led to the evolution of the symphony shaping the evolution of this earlier form—namely the developmental techniques and the ABA form derived from the fugue and the use of contrasting movements derived from the dance suite.

Sonatas for piano are the most numerous, with sonatas for violin and piano coming next, then cello and piano, flute and piano, clarinet and piano and finally almost any instrument you can think of. The two instruments are of equal importance; the piano is not relegated to mere accompaniment.

The piano sonatas of Haydn, Mozart, Beethoven, Schubert, Brahms and others form a basic literature for the piano. Beethoven alone wrote thirty-two sonatas including such well known masterpieces as the *Pathétique*, the *Appassionata* and the *Hammerklavier*. Mozart's *Sonata in C Major* has even been given a number of jazz or "pop" treatments so that its first theme is universally known. But perhaps the most familiar work in this category is the so-called *Moonlight Sonata* of Beethoven. The name *Moonlight* is, if anything, applicable only to the first movement (the popular part of the sonata) and is sometimes explained by a completely unauthenticated story about Beethoven having improvised it for a blind girl in a moonlit room. But he did call it a "Sonata in the style of a Fantasia" and he dedicated it to a woman he admired, the Countess Julie Guicciardi. The first movement does have a dreamlike quality in keeping with the word *fantasia* so one can understand how the story grew.

Should one analyze the *Moonlight Sonata,* bear in mind that it is unusual in that it begins with a slow movement (a small ABA form where B is in a rather free, improvisational style). The second movement is a not too rapid scherzo. The finale is in sonata-allegro form with three themes in the statement or exposition and is a very exciting movement.

All of the above mentioned composers wrote sonatas for violin and piano and most have also written them for cello and piano. Among the violin sonatas, the *Spring Sonata,* Opus 24 in F by Beethoven, lends itself readily to analysis because its especially beautiful melodies are easily remembered, differentiated and identified.

Sonatas are numerous in the works of Bach, Handel, Vivaldi and Corelli (Baroque composers), but these were forerunners of the Classical sonata and are largely contrapuntal in style and technique. We have limited our discussion of form to the Classical and Romantic composers whose sonatas, concertos, symphonies and overtures ran more often "true to form" so as not to confuse the listener.

So again may we remind the listener that the accurate discernment of the form is not important in and of itself, so long as intelligent listening makes one aware of how the composer is using, reusing and reshaping his materials.

In addition, form should not be thought of as inflexible or rigid. The great composers frequently broke away from the conventional patterns, sometimes with minor deviations and sometimes with significant changes. We mentioned the *Moonlight Sonata* which starts with a slow movement. Tchaikovsky's *Romeo and Juliet*, cited in Chapter XI, has a recapitulation that omits theme I largely because it is so much used in the development. So the recapitulation begins with the feud triumphant (theme II), the Friar (theme I) having been effectively smothered in the development section. And theme III (love) returns with the second part played before the first. Some works have special endings in place of what would normally be a coda, with entirely new material and some composers have even introduced new ideas in the development section. In analyzing a piece of music, therefore, one should not feel frustrated or think the composer has made a mistake if the piece does not fit neatly into the prescribed form. Exceptions abound.

XIII

SOME COMPOSERS AND THEIR
WORKS AND SOME HISTORY

BAROQUE AND CLASSICAL PERIODS

The greatest enjoyment of music comes directly from the music itself, and so we have tried to make the reader a "participant listener" by making him aware of the elements of music and of musical form. But this enjoyment can be further enriched by an understanding of the background of the music and the people who composed it.

The history of music is just another aspect of the history of man. We know how important music is (and was) to primitive man by observing how he uses it today in those remaining remote areas where civilization has not yet penetrated. And we know, too, from contemporary written accounts and from the preserved art of the period what part music played in earlier civilizations. In most cases we have few clues as to what such early music really sounded like because either music notation had not been developed or we cannot decipher it, and the art of recording had not been discovered.

It is only after a system of notation had been developed that we can trace the history of music in terms of the actual music—its changing styles, harmonies, instrumentation, etc. And, of course, it is only this music, which has been written down, that finds its way into the concert hall. Since we are concerned with the more standard concert repertoire we shall begin with the seventeenth century, arbitrarily omitting the long and important development of church music, the beginnings of opera, the beginnings and increasing importance of instrumental music—all of which are rewarding areas of further reading and investigation.

Naturally musical styles do not fit neatly into artificial designations

93

like centuries. All the dates and periods described are approximate and always overlap. In general, the seventeenth century which follows the Renaissance is known as the Baroque period (1600–1750). The late eighteenth century (actually 1770–1830) is referred to in music as the Classical period. A transition period which overlaps both periods is termed the Rococo (1725–1775). Unfortunately, the word Classical is used to mean many things and sometimes creates confusion. It frequently describes serious music regardless of when it was written as opposed to popular music (jazz, rock and roll, swing, etc.). It also refers to the ancient Greek and Roman civilizations and the inspiration they provided for the Renaissance.

The seventeenth and eighteenth centuries marked the culmination of the era of absolute monarchs as epitomized by the long reign of Louis XIV, and their subsequent weakening or decline, leading to revolution at the end of the period. Absolutism had produced courts of awesome magnificence in huge palaces, fantastically decorated in elaborate and frequently gaudy styles and it is to this ornate magnificence that the word Baroque refers. As the power of the absolute monarchs and the theory of rule by "divine right" faced increasing challenges from religious and political factions, mostly in the eighteenth century, court life also underwent changes. The magnificent and the ornate became elegant and over refined (and in the eyes of many historians, weaker and somewhat decadent) and it is to this refinement that the word Rococo refers.

After an early turning away from polyphony (many voices), the music of the Baroque period becomes heavily contrapuntal as in the Renaissance, but there is more use of the homophonic style (single melody with harmonic support). Its melodic lines are florid and elaborate and highly decorated with trills and grace notes. There is an inexorable quality to its rhythm—frequently pompous and even ponderous when slow, and relentlessly energetic when fast. Instrumental music, meagre in the earlier periods, now comes into its own, and composers show a greater interest in secular (non-sacred) music. In this era of magnificence at court we find a corresponding striving for the spectacular in music. We find Handel writing music for a bargeload of musicians to be played in a floating royal procession on the Thames (the famous *Water Music*), and Lully writing elaborate ballets in which King Louis XIV himself danced. Of course, this was the ideal climate for the beginnings of opera and oratorio.

The music of the Rococo period shows a much greater interest in the homophonic style and a corresponding falling off of the contrapuntal (which, however, never totally disappears). Melodies take on a greater lyricism and delicacy. As this period merges into the Classical era, the orchestra, though still small, assumes the shape of our present day symphony orchestra and instrumental music becomes even more important than in the Baroque period. The sonata-allegro form emerges and dominates instrumental music.

In both the Baroque and Classical periods, except for opera, other vocal music and ballet, the music was abstract (pure music) with a great deal of emphasis on form. Since much of the music was written to be performed at court or in church, it tended to be overly polite, avoiding emotional outbursts or unseemly passion which might disturb the king or the courtier or any other patron for whom it had been composed. This put the musician in the position of a paid servant catering to his master's taste and whims. But the skill and genius of many of the composers of the Classical period frequently broke through such superficial considerations of the patronage system and produced the masterpieces we cherish today.

Johann Sebastian Bach (*1685–1750*)

Sometimes called the father of modern music (as contrasted with music of earlier periods) Bach was a giant of the Baroque period. He seemed to have absorbed all that was good in the styles and techniques of composition that had flourished previously or were then developing not only in his native Germany, but in Italy, France and England as well, and this without ever traveling outside his own country or even much further than a hundred miles from his native town. He was invited briefly to the court of Frederick the Great and wrote some music for that monarch, but all of his life was spent in the service of the church and the local nobility. He was without question the greatest master of counterpoint and he brought the fugue to its highest point of perfection. He wrote hundreds of chorales (elaborate hymns) for use in Sunday services and achieved a harmonic fluency far surpassing that of the composers who had abandoned counterpoint for homophonic styles. He did much to advance the cause of tempered tuning of keyboard instruments, a new system of tuning that made possible greater freedom in changing key on such instruments without having to retune them (*The Well-Tempered Clavichord*). He was himself a virtuoso organist and composed many masterpieces for that instrument. He wrote orchestral suites, *concerti grossi* (the six *Brandenburg Concertos*), concertos for one, two and more harpsichords, concertos for violin and sonatas for a variety of instruments. He produced cantatas for all the church holidays as well as some secular ones, and he crowned all this with a number of truly monumental religious works for chorus, orchestra, and soloists. These include the *St. Matthew Passion*, the *Saint John Passion*, the *B Minor Mass* and the *Magnificat*. While these works are expressive and highly dramatic, Bach never tried his hand at opera.

Bach seemed perfectly happy with his lot under the patronage system. Certainly, whatever minor irritations his job held for him, they in no way interfered with his productivity, either musical or domestic. Twice married, Bach produced twenty children, the boys all becoming musicians, at least three of them of considerable fame and stature.

Bach was not really an innovator. Rather he was a traditionalist. But his skill and musical insights were so great and original that he rejuvenated old forms and enlivened them with the spark of genius. He was a truly religious man and was able to invest his church music with a devout intensity, reverent dignity and even a personal poignancy, rare in an age that frequently was content with abstract solemnity. His melodies are endlessly inventive and surprising, many of exceptional beauty. Vigorous and driving rhythms alternate with passages of immense tranquility or deep reflection.

Among his works we suggest the following for listening in addition to the *Little Fugue in G Minor* mentioned earlier:

Toccata and Fugue in D Minor for organ (or in orchestral transcription).
> The toccata is a tempestuous, even angry outburst. It is

followed by a magnificent fugue, based on an exciting subject which builds to a climax so shattering that it cannot end with just a last restatement of the subject, so Bach adds a very dramatic coda.

The *Overture in D Major* (Suite) which contains the famous *Air* (transcribed for violin solo as *Air on the G String*).

The *Suite in B Minor* for flute and strings which contains the lively and humorous *Badinerie*.

The *Concerto for Clavier* (Harpsichord or Piano) *in F minor*, the second movement of which has also become well known as a cello solo called *Arioso* and has an absolutely exquisite melody.

The *Cantata #140* containing the beautiful chorale *Wachet Auf* (*Sleepers Wake*).

The *Cantata #147* containing the well known and lovely chorale *Jesu Joy of Man's Desiring*.

St. Matthew Passion—especially the opening chorus and the very poignant double chorus at the end.

George Frederick Handel (1685–1759)

Handel was born the same year as Bach and like him suffered blindness at the end of his life. But in nearly every other respect the lives and output of the two men differed. Bach came from a long line of musicians whereas Handel's father was a barber-surgeon who wanted his son to be a lawyer. Bach spent his entire life in a small area of Germany dealing entirely with the local church officials and local relatively minor nobility. Handel traveled widely in Italy, England, Ireland and Holland and mixed with the great and near great wherever he went, enjoying the patronage of princes, kings and queens. He never married. He became a naturalized English citizen. He wrote vocal music to texts in four languages (German, Italian, English and Latin) while Bach wrote exclusively in German except for a few works in Latin including, of course, the great *B Minor Mass*. Handel wrote over forty operas and over thirty oratorios whereas Bach wrote no operas at all. Bach remained a contrapuntalist to the end although he occasionally wrote homophonically with a rich and varied harmonic texture. Handel was also a great contra-

97

puntalist (especially in choral writing) but his interest in opera led him to more homophonic styles (arias are, after all, accompanied songs) and his harmonic scheme was generally simpler and more square cut than Bach's. His interest in opera began in his teens and it is not surprising therefore that he produced far more secular than sacred music. Nevertheless, his crowning masterpiece is the oratorio *Messiah* based on biblical texts. It is a work of towering majesty and universal appeal and it is so straightforwardly devout and religious that it has earned for its composer the reputation of a church composer. But Handel turned to the composition of oratorios only after a very long career of writing operas, when popular taste in England switched from Italian-style opera to ballad-opera (*The Beggar's Opera*) and his own operas lost favor.

Handel as a young man had enjoyed an appointment as musician to the court of the Elector of Hanover in Germany but left Hanover for England where he found greater opportunities. Later, when the Elector of Hanover was invited to become King George I of England, Handel quickly won his way back into the king's favor and soon this German who wrote mostly Italian opera became the most respected and important English musician of his time. His adopted country honored him with burial in Westminster Abbey. In addition to operas and oratorios he wrote numerous cantatas. He was himself a fine organist and wrote concertos and other works for that instrument, as well as *concerti grossi,* concertos and sonatas for various instruments, and some harpsichord music.

Suggested for listening are:

The Oratorios:

Messiah (in whole or in part—contains some of the most thrilling choruses ever written including the great *Hallelujah Chorus* and some of the solo arias listed below).

Israel in Egypt and

Judas Maccabeas, the former because it enjoys more frequent performances than some of the other oratorios and the latter for the exciting *Hallelujah Amen* and *Hail the Conquering Hero Comes* choruses.

The operas are not so frequently produced these days, although

Julius Caesar has enjoyed a recent vogue. However, arias from various operas (and oratorios) appear on many concert programs and are examples of the beautiful melodic style which was Handel's and which featured the long unbroken line, sometimes florid, sometimes simple but always eloquent and dramatic.

Ombra mai fu (the popular *Largo*) from *Xerxes*
Affanni del pensier from *Ottone*
Ah! mio cor from *Alcina*
Lascia ch'io pianga from *Rinaldo*

are only a few of the better known operatic arias.

In the oratorios, such arias as these give further evidence of his lyric genius:

But who may abide
He shall feed his flock } from
I know that my Redeemer liveth } *Messiah*
Where'er you walk from *Semele*

Arrangements for modern symphony orchestra have been made of many movements of the *Water Music* and the *Firework Music* the most notable being the ones by Sir Hamilton Harty.

The harpsichord variations *The Harmonious Blacksmith* are delightfully melodious and very much in the Baroque style.

The *concerti grossi*, sonatas and chamber music are also worthy of attention and figure prominently in chamber music and solo programs.

We must not leave the reader with the impression that Bach and Handel who brought the Baroque period to a brilliant close were its only composers. Frescobaldi, the Scarlattis, Couperin, Rameau, Purcell, Corelli, Vivaldi, Telemann are names of composers whose music is constantly being played or sung. If, however, you have explored and enjoyed the music of Bach and Handel, you should find other Baroque music easy to understand.

Franz Joseph Haydn (1732–1809)

Of humble origin, Haydn was apprenticed as a choir boy in Vienna in early childhood, where he received some music education, but under circumstances that provided little parental love or care. By the time he was seventeen and his voice had changed, he was thrown entirely on his own. By teaching and playing he managed somehow to keep body and soul together and to continue learning his art. Soon he came to the attention of some minor nobility and eventually entered the service of the prominent, powerful and musically enthusiastic Esterhazy family in whose employ he remained full-time for over thirty years. Here his genius flowered and he produced many of the long succession of symphonies, string quartets and sonatas that helped to standardize the sonata-allegro form and which earned for him the respect and admiration of most of the great musicians of his time, particularly the young Mozart, and later, of Beethoven. The Esterhazys entertained distinguished guests from all the European capitals, and Haydn's fame spread, especially to Paris and London. When, finally, he visited London and spent some considerable time there, he was lionized by the public and honored with a doctorate from Oxford. He also produced twelve of his finest symphonies on this trip (the *London Symphonies*) including the popular *Surprise, Military, Drum Roll* and *Clock Symphonies*. Although he had already written operas, church music, oratorios and cantatas, his exposure to Handel's *Messiah* apparently inspired him to produce two masterpieces in oratorio form, *Creation* and *The Seasons*.

Controversy exists as to whether Haydn's ancestry was German or Croation (Croatia was a Slavic section of the Austro-Hungarian empire where Haydn was born). But there is no doubt that strong traces of Croation peasant or folk music can be found in his compositions. It is evident in the vigor of the dancelike rhythms that suffuse his work and the occasionally derivative and sometimes even "quoted" melodies. Something of the peasant earthiness remained with him all his life although he moved in the most refined circles. He was a fun-loving, hearty, good natured man, short and not very good looking, but very likable. He was so largely self-taught in composition, having learned by studying the works of other composers, that he was generous in his praise and admiration of competent colleagues. Except for a torturously unhappy marriage, he enjoyed the company and sometimes the favors of the opposite sex. He had no children of his own, but he lavished a paternal affection on his pupils and co-workers who referred to him as "Papa Haydn." Much of his music reflects this open, warm and sunny disposition. Even in his church works, and Haydn was a devout Christian, his religion is optimistic and promising rather than somber and solemn. Yet he is capable of tenderness.

His output was enormous—over one hundred symphonies, more than eighty string quartets, numerous trios and other chamber music, concertos, sonatas, operas, oratorios, cantatas, songs, and even shows for Count Esterhazy's marionette theatre. His earliest instrumental works were written for almost any combination of whatever instruments were available. As his competence and reputation grew, and he could command larger groups, he enlarged his instrumental scope. Not only did he set the standard for instrumentation, but, as already mentioned, he made such increasingly effective use of the new sonata -allegro form that his symphonies became, and are still regarded as, the model Classical symphonies. His favoring and skillful handling of the minuet assured it of its place as the third movement in the four movement symphonic sequence. What he did for the symphony he also did for the string quartet, shaping its form and giving it ever increasing clarity while at the same time writing always more individualized parts for the four instruments.

In addition to the symphonies already cited (they are named for some obvious feature in the work like the sudden *fortissimo* chord in the quietest section of the slow movement of the *Surprise Symphony* which was supposed to awaken anyone who might have fallen asleep during the music) we suggest for further listening:

String Quartet in D, Opus 64 #5 (*The Lark*) and
String Quartet in C, Opus 76 #3 (*The Emperor*)—the second
    movement is a theme and variations based on the marvelous
    tune Haydn composed for the Austrian National Anthem.
The magnificent *The Heavens are Telling* from the *Creation* is
    one of the great choral masterpieces of all time.
The *Piano Sonatas B & H #35 in C* (Breitkopf and Härtel—
    German publishing firm that catalogued Haydn's works) and
    B & H #37 in D are favorites among students of the piano.

Wolfgang Amadeus Mozart (1756–1791)

Mozart is undoubtedly one of the most amazing examples of natural-born genius the world has ever known. His musical gift was clearly manifested when he was only three years old. His father, Leopold, himself an accomplished musician and teacher, seems to have known full well how to foster and develop it. When he was six, Mozart and his ten year old sister, Nannerl, also very musical, were taken by their father on a concert tour of the capitals of Europe. The children astounded audiences with their performing ability, but Wolfgang was the more remarkable, playing both harpsichord and violin, featuring his own compositions as well as works of others, and improvising music on the spur of the moment. He attracted so much attention as a child prodigy, that his father took him on a series of such trips spending time in Paris, London, the major cities of Italy and, of course, Holland, Belgium and many German and Austrian cities. The young Mozart met most of the prominent musicians of the day, all of whom were greatly impressed by the *wunderkind* (wonderful child). But, what was more important, the boy seemed to absorb musical experience and knowledge like a blotter absorbs ink. He also found time, in spite of the strenuous schedule and the grinding hardships of travel in the eighteenth century, to compose incessantly, producing his first symphonies at the age of eight, piano concertos at eleven, an opera at thirteen and numerous smaller works for keyboard instruments, violin, voice and orchestra.

Inevitably the time came when Mozart was no longer a sensational child prodigy, but a young man. While his genius was recognized, especially among other musicians, he no longer attracted as much attention, so he settled, not too happily, into the service of the rather unsympathetic Prince-Archbishop of Salzburg, Mozart's birthplace. He continued to compose at a prodigious rate with ever increasing skill and maturity. But the Archbishop was resentful of the commissions and honors coming to Mozart from places outside Salzburg. Continuing friction eventually led to Mozart's resignation from the Archbishop's service. Though he tried repeatedly, he was never able to win another post in the service of any of the more important Austrian or other nobility, and he was forced to live on what he could earn from teaching and individual commissions (music ordered for special occasions or for particular individuals). This, coupled with marriage to a woman who was a notoriously poor manager and who bore him six children, only two of whom survived, kept him desperately impoverished and in debt for the rest of his short life. Nor was Mozart himself very wise in handling money, frequently letting it slip through his fingers in some silly extravagance.

Poverty and misfortune, however, did little to dampen his creativity. On the contrary, some of Mozart's most masterful compositions stem from the last years of his life when his situation seemed utterly hopeless and when he was literally reduced to begging his friends for handouts. He died from what historians have variously described as exhaustion, malnutrition or frail health, broken perhaps, by the strenuous and exhausting travels of his youth, but more likely by the precarious poverty of his maturity. He was composing a Requiem Mass at the time of his death, and although the work had been commissioned, he was convinced it was to be his own requiem. There was no money for a proper funeral so he was buried in an unmarked pauper's grave, the exact location of which has never been discovered.

In a lifetime of thirty-five years, twenty-nine of them actively devoted to composing, Mozart produced over 600 works (as catalogued by Köchel). He wrote in every conceivable category and excelled in all of them. While he was capable of turning out music at a furious rate, it was always polished, elegant and graceful. Mozart was no intellectual, and he seemed little moved by the social ferment of the end of the eighteenth century. But we know he resented the patronage system and that he was attracted to the high and rather democratic ideals of Freemasonry; he even became a Freemason. (This was a fraternal order based on principles of equality, religious toleration and peace.) His later works may reflect some of these ideals in their increased strength and dramatic intensity and assertiveness; never is there a loss of elegance, however.

Having already analyzed the *Symphony #40 in G Minor*, the

reader should also explore Mozart's *Haffner Symphony #35* and his last work in this form, the *Jupiter Symphony #41*—all are considered among the greatest works ever written in this form.

Mozart claimed that he learned how to write a string quartet properly from Haydn, and his later quartets are sometimes referred to as the Haydn set, any one of which would amply repay further listening and analysis. The piano concertos are also extremely rewarding, especially *K.467 in C Major* (with its dreamily romantic slow movement), *K.488 in A Major* (with its hauntingly lovely second movement in a minor key), the very dramatic *K.491 in C Minor* and, of course, *K.537 in D Major*, the well known *Coronation Concerto*, so called because Mozart played it at the Coronation of Leopold II in 1790, though he had not composed it for that occasion. Mozart performed outstandingly on both the violin and the piano (though he preferred the latter instrument) and his *Violin Concerto, K. 219 in A Major* is a very popular work. A little more unusual, but masterpieces in their own right are the *Concerto for Two Pianos in E flat (K.365)* and the *Sinfonia Concertante in E flat for Violin and Viola (K.364)*. Mozart also wrote concertos for bassoon, flute, clarinet and a whole series for horn.

The many sonatas for solo piano and for violin and piano figure frequently on the recital stage, as do the many chamber works such as piano trios, piano quartets (we have already mentioned the *Clarinet Quintet*), *Divertimenti, Serenades* (the most famous of these being the *Eine Kleine Nachtmusik K.525*) and various other instrumental combinations.

Mozart wrote a great deal of vocal music including much music for the church—masses, *Kyries, Te Deums*, motets, offertoriums, and, of course, the great *Requiem Mass*. But the works of which he was probably proudest and which, he hoped, would bring him greatest fame and honor were his operas. They form a continuous string through his composing years beginning when he was twelve with *La Finta Semplice* and ending, in the last year of his life, with *The Magic Flute* and *La Clemenza di Tito*. The current repertoire of the world's great opera companies includes more operas by Mozart than by any of his contemporaries or predecessors, most of whose works are now considered too "dated" or old fashioned for modern tastes.

The Marriage of Figaro and Don Giovanni are perhaps his most popular works, but Cosi fan tutte and The Magic Flute are close behind and The Escape from the Seraglio and Idomeneo are frequently performed. His dramatic range is remarkable, stretching from the farcical moments in Figaro, Cosi, and Seraglio, through the pageantry and ritual of The Magic Flute to the tensions and tragedy of Don Giovanni. The characterizations and the music have a humanity, a sly humor, a tenderness and a passion rarely achieved in that era of formal elegance, where refinement of form and technique was generally more emphasized than the actual musical material. It is precisely this ability of Mozart's to imbue his music with so much humanity and feeling while at the same time achieving such heights of refinement and such brilliance of technique, that proclaims his genius and crowns the whole Classical period.

We must stress that the Classical period does not consist exclusively of music by Haydn and Mozart. Other names you may encounter on concert programs are Boccherini, Gluck (who did much to reform opera), Bach's sons—Karl Philipp Emanuel Bach, Wilhelm Friedmann Bach, and Johann Christian Bach, also von Dittersdorf and the Stamitzs, father and sons, sometimes referred to as The Mannheim School since they were associated with a very fine orchestra in that city.

*　　*　　*

Ludwig van Beethoven—A Transition—(1770–1827)

Beethoven was born in Bonn, Germany. His father was a court singer, an irascible man given to drink, who, in the hope that his son was sufficiently gifted, had visions of exploiting him as another child prodigy like Mozart. He subjected the boy to a cruel schedule of training by mostly mediocre teachers, but was unable to launch him as a spectacular *wunderkind*. Meanwhile, Ludwig quit formal schooling when he was eleven, lost his mother when he was sixteen, and, because of his father's drunkenness, was made legal head of his family when he was eighteen. It is a miracle that he was able to develop either musically or intellectually under such circumstances. Yet by this time he had already met Mozart who predicted he would some day "make a noise in the world." To support himself he played viola in a theatre orchestra. He secured some pupils, and through them formed some valuable friendships with important people. When, a few years later, he met Haydn who invited him to come to Vienna and study with him, these friendships served as a warm introduction to Viennese society. Haydn, busy with his own career, turned out to be a less than diligent teacher and Beethoven secretly studied with others.

Meagerly educated and lacking the manners and sophistication of the circles in which he moved, Beethoven was nevertheless accepted by them on a basis quite different from the patronage that had prevailed earlier. Where Bach, Haydn, and to a slightly lesser extent, Handel and Mozart were highly valued, appreciated and even honored servants, Beethoven was treated as a respected artist. Perhaps this was because times were changing. Beethoven was six when the American revolution broke out and nineteen when the French revolution shook the very foundations of European aristocracy and gave dignity to the citizen, "the common man." Beethoven identified very closely with "the common man" and with democratic ideals, instinctively valuing his own ability more highly than "blue blood." Hot tempered, moody, given to extremes of affection and anger, often crude, personally untidy and unkempt, he was not an easy person to like. Yet he never lacked devoted friends. He undertook the guardianship of his brother's son, Karl, but his affection and care were wasted on a ne'r-do-well. His frequent and passionate loves were seldom reciprocated. He never married. But the crushing tragedy of his life was his deafness. First noticed when he was about twenty-eight, it became progressively worse over the next ten or fifteen years, gradually making it impossible for him to perform and forcing people to communicate with him only in writing. Fortunately, it did not stop him from composing. One wonders whether the later works would have emerged differently had he been able to hear them in reality as well as in his mind.

Beethoven's work falls into three periods. The early works show the strong influence of his teacher, Haydn, and of Mozart, but with clear indications of an independent style. The use of the orchestra is bolder, movements are longer, developments more inventive, introductions more original, and third movements have changed from minuets to scherzos. The middle period produced his best known and most popular works, larger in emotional scope and size, works of monumental strength. The late works take on an introspective quality and point in new and very advanced directions, even judged by today's standards.

At a time when counterpoint was becoming less important, Beethoven, who had given it only occasional attention at first, proves himself in these later works to be a master contrapuntalist. He attempted to unify the multi-movement work by quoting or repeating in later movements themes previously used, or by deriving new thematic material from one common idea or "germ" motive. Such works are called "cyclic" or "generic." He loved nature and often achieved an "outdoors" effect, sometimes pastoral and sometimes tempestuous, that seldom figured in the music of his predecessors. He could build tremendous tensions in his music—struggles of anger, passion and philosophy. And he could produce a celestial tranquility. Everything from inspired exaltation to searing tragedy, from the hunt and country dances to the formal minuet, or to a towering rage, flowed from his pen. Unlike the earlier Classicists who only rarely strayed from the polite detachment of the courtly or "gallant" style, Beethoven could be intimate and speak directly to his listener, or universal and speak to the whole world, regardless of class distinction. It is this infusion into music of the personal element with all its emotional riches that makes Beethoven the bridge between Classicism and the Romanticism that was to mark the nineteenth century. In a sense he "democratized" music, moving it from the palace to the concert hall. Of course, revolution—political, industrial, intellectual and even religious—had made the time ripe for the change, but Beethoven met the challenge heroically.

He was a deliberate and painstaking worker. The notebooks he kept show that he made preliminary sketches for works that took final shape years after the first sketches. Nonetheless, he produced a formidable number of works, a great many of which form the backbone of the present day concert repertoire.

He wrote nine symphonies, all masterpieces, the odd numbered more popular than the even. The *Fifth Symphony in C Minor,*

Opus 67, is probably the best known of all symphonies. Beethoven is said to have called its opening motive, with its three short and one long note, the "Fate" motive. Certainly it has all the ominous power of fate, and all the strength of the victory that the motive has come to symbolize for the generations since World War II. The original dedication for the *Third Symphony in Eb Major, Opus 55* was to Napoleon for spreading the democratic ideals of the French revolution, but when Napoleon declared himself Emperor, Beethoven changed the dedication to "a hero" and it has since been known as the *Eroica Symphony*. The *Ninth Symphony in D Minor, Opus 125*, is called the *Choral Symphony* because in its last movement it calls for vocal soloists and a large chorus which Beethoven felt was necessary for the musical expression of his great ideal of the brotherhood of man. His love of nature found expression in the *Pastoral*, the *Sixth Symphony in F Major, Opus 68*, where he describes a day in the country including a sudden storm, one of the earliest examples of symphonic tone-painting. His five piano concertos are constantly performed and rank as the finest examples of the form, as does the violin concerto which we analyzed. We also mentioned the thirty-two piano sonatas, the violin and cello sonatas and the marvelous chamber music (especially the quartets and trios) in the chapter on chamber music (Chapter XII).

Beethoven wrote one opera, *Fidelio*, which is still performed all over the world. For it he wrote four overtures, three of them known by the name of the heroine of the opera, Leonore. The opera deals with the brave efforts of a faithful wife to save her husband from death as a political prisoner. In it, Beethoven idealizes a conjugal love he was never to experience. He also wrote a *Missa Solemnis* (*Solemn Mass*), a large, intensely and dramatically devout work, as well as a large number of songs including the lovely song cycle *An die ferne Geliebte* (*To a Distant Beloved*). He composed a ballet, *The Creatures of Prometheus* and incidental music to a number of stage works including Goethe's drama, *Egmont*. This leads us to a consideration of his treatment of the overture, a form he elevated to full symphonic stature. Composed, for the most part, in strict sonata-allegro form without ever losing sight of dramatic tensions, the *Egmont Overture* is a summary statement of Goethe's historical tale of Flemish rebellion against Spanish domination and the Inquisition. Similarly, the *Leonore Overture #3* so effectively outlines the motivation and conflicts of the opera *Fidelio* that it is never played before the opera, but rather as an entr'acte before the last act. To play it first would be to give away too much. The *Coriolanus Overture* inspired not by Shakespeare, but by a German play on the same subject, is another such work. All these overtures have become concert favorites and have set the standard for the concert overture.

Beethoven's unpredictable and rebellious nature shows through in the wide range and sudden changes in the dynamics of his music. Exciting *crescendos* build to abrupt hushes of whispering softnesses. Crashing chords, sometimes aggressive, sometimes majestic, yield to subdued echoes or give way to quiet melodies. Naturally, all this called for greater flexibility in handling the orchestra. Beethoven enlarged it by adding more strings from which he could draw a much warmer tone and which he needed to balance an enlarged wind section. He used the full woodwind quartet in pairs (two flutes, two oboes, two clarinets and two bassoons) and a fuller brass section consisting often of four French horns, two trumpets and occasionally three trombones. He gave much more important and independent parts to the double basses and to the timpani and challenged all the instruments technically, both in solo and ensemble passages.

In short, in spite of the blight of deafness, he enlarged every aspect of his art with imagination and new concepts of liberty and emotional freedom.

ROMANTIC PERIOD (1820–1900)

Indirectly, Napoleon was almost as important in establishing the new feelings of individual worth and emotional freedom we refer to as "Romanticism" as was Beethoven and the many revolutions we mentioned. Appearing at first to be the great emancipator (he was to spread the benefits of the French Revolution over all of Europe), but then shifting to the role of conqueror (after declaring himself Emperor), he caused people to rise to the defense of their homelands. This, in turn, fanned the fires of patriotism. Coupled with the growing democratization, economic betterment and increased literacy of many of the poorer classes, patriotism blossomed into a fervor of nationalism that found glorious musical expression in the second half of the Romantic period. National pride sent authors and poets as well as musicians searching into the national heritage of folklore and history. This had happened before, when, during the Renaissance and the Classical periods, artists sought inspiration from ancient Greece and Rome. But in the nineteenth century they rediscovered the Medieval period and the Age of Chivalry with its lofty ideals and romantic heroes and heroines as well as its magic, both good and evil, its supernatural figures such as witches, ghosts and dragons, its mysticism—all very subjective stuff. And subjectivity (in contrast to the formal objectivity of the Classic period) is the essence of Romanticism. Music became more programmatic, concerning itself with nature, love, adventure—all things close to the heart and interests of ordinary people. No longer was it the decorative adornment of a richly mannered life-style or the beautiful, dignified handmaiden of religion. Instead it was the intimately personal expression of the hopes, fears, pleasures, pains, dreams and imaginings of each of us.

In Germany especially it seized on the outpourings of the Romantic poets, Goethe, Heine, Schiller and gave us the *"lied"* (art song) which ranges from miniature musings on nature, love, death, etc. to complete though short dramas (see *Erlking* analysis—Chapter VI). An instrumental counterpart, a short piece, usually for piano with descriptive titles like *Nocturne, Ballade, Intermezzo, Capriccio, Rhapsody, Impromtu, Romance, Fantasy, Prelude,* became popular. These were generally lyrical and poetic or dazzlingly brilliant, almost songs without words. (See Chapter VI—Poetry and Music—Song and Small Forms.)

The larger forms, following Beethoven's lead, grew larger, freer in form, generally more expressive and frequently programmatic. The preoccupation with story or descriptive elements led to the development of new forms such as the concert overture, the symphonic poem (or tone poem) and the symphonic suite. The first two of these are single movement works. The overture usually follows sonata—allegro form to some extent, but frequently outlines a story or event or describes a place. The symphonic poem does just about the same thing, but its form is dictated by its program rather than by any strict adherence to sonata form. The symphonic suite is a collection of several tone poems all dealing with some common or unifying idea (See Chapter VIII—Program Music, for example).

Beethoven's larger orchestra proved to be only a beginning. As noted in Chapter V, mechanical improvement in the fingering systems used on the various woodwind instruments and the invention of the valve system for brass instruments greatly increased their technical possibilities. As composers began to exploit them, they used more of these instruments, always adding more strings to balance the added winds. In the percussion section, the awakening interest in national and folk music called for characteristic instruments such as castanets, tambourines, cymbals, Oriental gongs etc. Interest in magic and mysticism set composers to devising all kinds of special effects, using mutes (devices for softening, and often completely changing the tone of an instrument), as well as tinkling bells, sonorous chimes, rattles, wind machines—whatever was necessary to create the desired mood or atmosphere. Sometimes, bigness became an end in itself and we find works calling for huge orchestras, several large choruses and many soloists.

Instrumental improvements were by no means limited to the wind instruments. The strings, already brought to a virtuoso level by improvements in earlier periods (Stradivari *et al.*) were given a further push by improvements in the design of the bow made by Tourte (1747–1835). (See Chapter V.) Keyboard instruments underwent a drastic change with the invention of the piano usually attributed to Cristofori (1665–1731). Although the first pianos appeared early in the eighteenth century it was some considerable time before they began to supplant their predecessors, the harpsichord (and its variations—spinet, clavecin, cembalo, virginal) and the clavichord. These earlier instruments used the keyboard to activate quills or tangents that plucked or pressed the string. Notes could not be sustained nor could they be varied dynamically. The piano, with a hammer action, could make a note either soft (*piano*) or loud (*forte*) depending on the amount of force with which a key was depressed. Hence the name piano-forte, generally shortened to piano. At first the piano used the harpsichord and clavichord litera-

111

ture. Bach would not write for it. But Mozart and Beethoven did, as did all the composers of the Romantic period.

Improved instruments, large public audiences, and highly emotional music produced a great many virtuosos, especially violinists and pianists (see Chapter V), and virtuosity was one of the characteristics of the Romantic period.

* * *

EARLY ROMANTIC COMPOSERS

Franz Schubert (1797–1828)

Born in Vienna to a struggling schoolmaster, Schubert was given his first music lessons by his father, brother and the local church choirmaster. He learned as much as they could teach him in very short order, so it was fortunate that by the time he was eleven years old he was accepted as one of the choristers in the Imperial Chapel, a post that provided for a strict, but reasonably good education, with lots of music thrown in including some instruction from Salieri, Mozart's chief rival. But when his voice changed at sixteen, he left the post like Haydn, and at his father's insistence entered a normal school to qualify as a teacher. He taught elementary school for about three years until he was twenty, and he seemed to hate every minute of it because it interfered with his composing which was literally continual. His first works were instrumental, then choral. He developed an interest in opera which was to last throughout his brief life, but none of his theatrical pieces has held the stage. However, great songs poured forth in a seemingly endless stream. Among the hundreds he wrote in addition to those already mentioned in earlier chapters, such masterpieces as *Ave Maria, Who is Sylvia?, Ständchen* (the famous *Serenade*), *Hark, Hark, the Lark, Tod und das Mädchen* (*Death and the Maiden*) and *Heidenröslein* would have insured his immortality had he written nothing else. Three of his symphonies figure constantly in concert programs—the charming, almost classic *Fifth Symphony in Bb Major* written when he was only nineteen, the *Unfinished Symphony* which probably along with Beethoven's

Fifth ranks as the most often played symphony, and the great *Seventh Symphony in C Major,* "of heavenly length." These last two works have much of the power and grandeur of Beethoven, whom Schubert worshipped.

Schubert attracted a group of very devoted and musical friends and this Schubertian circle was instrumental in safeguarding and cataloguing his many works as well as frequently providing him with food and lodging. Schubert, himself, was not a well organized person. The *Unfinished Symphony* remained unfinished because he sent the two movements to a friend, then got interested in other compositions and lost track of it. Nor was this the only work he neglected to finish. In his dealings with publishers he was generally cheated since he had no mind for business. His Schubertian circle arranged most of the performances of his works, frequently performing themselves, especially the songs and chamber music. Although this group provided him with praise and encouragement, it would seem that Schubert achieved a rather limited recognition in his lifetime, certainly less than any of the "greats" we have thus far mentioned. He died in 1828 at the age of thirty-one, probably of typhus. But it wasn't until 1888 when Vienna decided to enshrine its great composers, that Schubert and Beethoven were reburied side by side in the Central Cemetery. Fame came posthumously to Schubert. The *Unfinished Symphony* composed in 1822 was first performed in 1865 nor did Schubert ever hear the *C Major Symphony* which Schumann gave its first performance long after Schubert's death.

Notable among his other works and particularly attractive are the *Trout Quintet* (*Die Forellen*) which includes a theme and variations movement based on the song we mentioned in chapter VI, the *Death and the Maiden Quartet,* also using one of his songs, some of the piano sonatas, and, of course, the *Marches Militaires* (piano, four hands) and the *Rosamunde Overture.*

EARLY ROMANTIC OPERA

Opera, like the rest of music, felt the invigorating push of Romanticism. From its very beginnings in 1600 until the present day, opera has always presented a problem of balance between the various elements that go into it. Is the plot more important than the music or the music more important than the plot? Is the singer more important than either of the two? Claudio Monteverdi in the seventeenth century, Christoph Willibald von Gluck in the eighteenth century, Carl Maria von Weber in the early nineteenth century, and later Richard Wagner are among the composers who consciously strove to achieve what each considered a proper balance. They did exert a considerable influence on operatic form and style and each achieved great popularity in his own time, but with the exception of Wagner few of their works are still performed. Monteverdi's operas (mostly his *Orfeo*) are occasionally revived out of historical interest. Gluck, whose reforms included a return to simpler plots and less florid vocal techniques enjoyed great popularity in his own day, but only his *Orfeo e Euridice* is performed with any frequency today. Carl Maria von Weber (1786–1826) however, had a wider influence. In the first place he was a German writing German opera (Mozart had written mostly in Italian although *The Magic Flute* and *Seraglio* were written in German.) Secondly, he was much interested in folk music and this shows up in his chorus writing especially in *Der Freischütz*. His plots were definitely of the romantic school, full of magic, mystery and chivalry in addition to a budding Germanic strength and pride. His melodies were bold, brilliant and passionate, as was his use of the orchestra. While his operas are hardly the mainstays of the repertoire, *Der Freischütz* and *Oberon* and especially their overtures are still performed with some frequency. In his brief life of forty years, he managed to establish German opera as a worthy counterpart to the dominant Italian opera of the early nineteenth century, and to point the way to Wagner and Strauss.

Meanwhile Italian opera continued to develop in ways not much influenced by the reformers. A style called *"bel canto"* (beautiful song) prevailed and the balance weighed heavily in favor of the singer and virtuosity. Opera *buffa* (comic opera) featured complicated and often silly plots with much opportunity for exaggerated clowning. Such an opera is Rossini's *Barber of Seville*. Opera *seria* (tragic opera) was often bloody and violent with heroines going mad as in Donizetti's *Lucia di Lammermoor*. But comic or tragic, they had to be full of great solo arias and brilliant duets, trios and larger ensemble numbers. The style remains popular and quite a few of Rossini's, (1792–1868) Donizetti's (1797–1848) as well as Bellini's (1801–1835) operas, such as *Norma*, are regulars in all the opera houses of the world.

Early nineteenth century French opera is dominated by Giacomo Meyerbeer (1791–1864) whose operas such as *Le Prophet* and *L'Africaine* were spectacular, usually historical, and included ballets, all in deference to the specific demands and taste of the Paris public. But the giants of opera, Verdi and Wagner, were yet to come, and we will deal with them along with the other late Romanticists.

Felix Mendelssohn (1809–1847)

Aptly named Felix, which means happy or fortunate, Mendelssohn was born into a family of means and culture. Like Mozart, both Felix and his sister showed considerable talent at a very early age and their talent was carefully and intelligently nurtured by loving parents. The Mendelssohn's house was a gathering place for artists, writers and musicians of some importance and so the children were exposed to lively intellectual stimulation. The family travelled some and beginning in his teens, Felix travelled more. He met and became a good friend of Goethe, though he was only twelve years old and the old poet-philosopher was in his seventies. He attended the University of Berlin and then, at the age of twenty, toured Europe for three years, moving always in the company of the great musicians of the day. He was an excellent pianist, organist and conductor and frequently performed during his travels. But many of the places he visited made very deep impressions on the sensitive and receptive young composer and he left us a legacy of delightful musical souvenirs. A trip to Scotland inspired the overture *Fingal's Cave* (described in Chapter XI) and the *Scotch Symphony* while a stay in Italy brought forth the *Italian Symphony*. All of these works as well as the incidental music he composed for Shakespeare's *Midsummer Night's Dream* have a wonderfully "outdoorsy" kind of quality. Leaves rustle, winds whisper, long vistas stretch away into the distance, night falls and darkness deepens into dreams (as in the lovely

Nocturne from *Midsummer Night's Dream*) peasants dance and wood sprites scamper in hidden places. It is this ability to catch these aspects of nature, along with a penchant for graceful and appealing melody, that makes Mendelssohn important among the early Romanticists, since in matters of form he remained quite conservative and classical. His use of strings and woodwinds in the orchestra is especially colorful and imaginative, sometimes quite daring and reckless in fast movements.

By the time he was sixteen he had completed a comic opera, and his great and beautiful *Octet for Strings, Opus 20*. At seventeen he wrote the masterful *Overture to Midsummer Night's Dream*. He wrote the rest of the incidental music for the play including the now traditional *Wedding March* seventeen years later, but the style of the Overture was so perfect and so appropriate that he took great pains to match it in the later music.

Mendelssohn wrote two oratorios, *St. Paul* and *Elijah*, the second of which ranks as one of the masterpieces in that form. In all likelihood he was inspired to write these when he arranged to perform Bach's *St. Matthew Passion*, a work neglected and forgotten since its performances during Bach's lifetime. So successful were these performances that they established Mendelssohn's reputation as a conductor and rekindled an interest in Bach's music—a spark which Mendelssohn fanned throughout his life.

He was invited to be permanent conductor of the Leipzig Gewandhaus Orchestra, in those days one of Europe's outstanding orchestras. He excited so much enthusiasm that he was asked to organize the Leipzig Conservatory of Music, destined to become one of the truly important music schools of the world.

He was very happily married, but enjoyed very close ties to his family and suffered greatly at the deaths of his parents. When his sister, Fanny, died the loss was even more terrible since he shared so much of his musical life with her. His health began to fail, but he continued a very heavy schedule of work, composing, conducting, teaching and playing. He died at the age of thirty-eight and was mourned not only in Germany, but in Paris and London and all over Europe.

Three symphonies besides those previously mentioned, much

chamber music, two piano concertos and what is probably the most loved of all violin concertos, the *Violin Concerto in E Minor* round out the list of his major works.

He wrote much piano music, especially in small forms, and these pieces he called *Songs Without Words*. The most famous of these is the *Spring Song*. But he also set many texts by the German Romantic poets as well as some by English poets. His best known song is *On Wings of Song*.

His short but happy life left us with music that sparkles with joy and vitality, that sings with feeling and in *Elijah* reaches profundity.

Robert Schumann (1810-1856)

Schumann's father was a bookseller and editor, which probably accounts for the son's musical interests extending not only to composition but to criticism as well. He, like Mendelssohn, was a champion of the music of Bach. He discovered the manuscript and arranged for Mendelssohn to perform the great *C Major Symphony* by Schubert; he recognized the worth and had high praise for Chopin and for Berlioz and he "discovered" the young Brahms. For many years he edited a journal on music which crusaded for higher standards both in composition and performance.

He made an effort to study law, but with the encouragement of his piano teacher (who later, very unwillingly, became his father-in-law) he turned his entire attention to music. He had hoped to be a great pianist. However, in an attempt to strengthen his fourth finger and improve his technique he invented a gadget that only succeeded in crippling his hand, so all his energies went into composition.

Robert fell in love with his piano teacher's daughter, Clara Wieck, who showed early promise of becoming one of the great pianists of her day. And since he, too, had entertained such ambitions, his early works were mostly piano compositions. In much of this music he engages in a kind of musical satire, contrasting his own high standards of originality and imagination with the all too fashionable triteness and mediocrity he found so prevalent. Such works are *Carnaval* with its musical portraits of Schumann's friends and acquaintances and the *Davidsbündlertänze* (*Dances of the David*

Society—as in David against the Philistines, symbolic of Schumann's struggle against the forces of musical stagnation). Many collections of short pieces such as Fantasiestücke (Fantasy Pieces), Nachtstücke (Night Pieces), and some sonatas now comprise a major and very important segment of the concert pianist's repertoire.

Robert's courtship of Clara (one of music history's great love stories) and the early years of his marriage produced a raft of beautiful songs, many of them, like Widmung (Dedication) such passionate and personal outpourings that they seem to epitomize Romanticism. Clara's father had objected to the marriage, not without some justification as it turned out, on the grounds that a composer was not likely to be a "good provider." As the family grew the pressures of providing were in fact shared by Clara, who fortunately was in demand as a virtuoso. It was through her frequent performances of Robert's compositions that his reputation increased. Schumann, however, never suffered from poverty and the family always lived comfortably.

Though well educated, Schumann had little formal training in music. He soon outgrew the piano lessons available in the small town where he lived until of college age. His father died when Robert was quite young and his mother opposed a musical career so little more was done until finally, at the age of twenty, he became a full-time musician. Then he began serious study of piano and composition, but he was already largely self-taught and in many respects, very advanced and original. When he turned his attention to the orchestra, however, his handling of instruments was not as adroit as his treatment of the piano. Nevertheless, he wrote four great symphonies, a stunningly beautiful Piano Concerto in A Minor and a Cello Concerto all of which figure prominently in today's programming. Some interesting chamber music, choral works with and without orchestra, and one opera round out his compositions.

While he was given to expressing himself readily and well in writing, Schumann would frequently sit silent, even in the company of friends. As he grew older, he withdrew more and became something of a recluse or "loner." Although he adored his wife and children, and was always a thoughtful and generous friend, these periods of withdrawal became more frequent and increasingly melancholic, eventually resulting in his jumping from a bridge into the Rhine in an unsuccessful suicide attempt. He died in Clara's arms at the age of forty-six, having spent his last two years in a private asylum—a tragic end for a really lovable man so much of whose music is so full of joy, vigor, tenderness and humor.

Frédéric Chopin (1810–1849)

The Polish born son of a French father and a Polish mother, Chopin reflected this double heritage in his life and his music. He left war-torn Poland when he was about twenty years old and after some wandering settled more or less permanently in Paris. He had enjoyed a great vogue among the Polish aristocracy as a child prodigy who not only played the piano beautifully, but improvised with astonishing skill. He began composing early under the rather benign guidance of the head of the Warsaw Conservatory, Elsner, who recognized a strikingly original talent and was reluctant to discipline it for fear of destroying it. The rest of his schooling was not distinguished in any way. Although he was very shy, he had a taste for elegance in clothes and manners, and since his Polish friends equipped him with letters of introduction to influential Parisians it wasn't long before he was enjoying the company of Mendelssohn, Liszt, and Rossini, playing piano at fashionable soirées in the homes of the wealthy and giving piano lessons to rich ladies at high fees. One would think that little music of value could come from such an existence. But Chopin was suffering from homesickness (an ailment that was to remain chronic throughout the rest of his life) and many compositions in Polish styles or rhythms give evidence of this. *Mazurkas, Polonaises, Krakowiak, Grande Fantasie on Polish Airs* are examples. Then, too, he was a young man living alone away from parental influences in one of the world's most exciting and romantic cities. While he was no Don Juan he did become involved with the Baroness Dudevant, a novelist better known by her pseudonym, George Sand. Many women writers assumed masculine names since men fared better in the publishing world, but George Sand went further and frequently wore men's clothing. Theirs was not an easy romance for she was the more aggressive and stronger personality, while he was more sensitive and easily hurt. Nevertheless it endured for several years during which time she nursed him through a number of critical illnesses. When, after their separation, Chopin was in his final illness, she came to pay her respects, but he would not see her.

So while he seemed frail and delicate and moved in a polite and mannered world, Chopin's inner life was full of turmoil and deeply felt emotion. He wrote almost exclusively for the piano, rarely utilizing and never really mastering the orchestra. Nor did he show much interest in program music, turning out many abstract small forms which he called *Preludes, Nocturnes, Impromptus, Etudes, Waltzes* and the Polish styles already mentioned. But a superb gift for melody and an ability to move harmonically from key to key with the endless and fascinating variety of a kaleidoscope lifted most of his work far above the level of mere prettiness. He employed and invented highly original piano styles demanding great technical facility, exploiting the keyboard and the pedal in hitherto unexplored ways. And he permitted a kind of rhythmic flexibility called *rubato* that lent a dimension of spontaneity to his music. The result is a catalogue of pianistic masterpieces. Some of his works are in large forms. There are two fine piano concertos in E and F minor, some piano sonatas, one for cello and piano and a string trio. He ranges from the delicate grace and sheer transparency of some of the *Waltzes* and *Mazurkas* through the fanciful flights of the *Scherzos* and *Impromptus* and the passionate heroics of the *Ab Polonaise*, the *G Minor Ballade* and the *Revolutionary Etude* to the ultimate tragedy of the slow movement (*Funeral March*) of the *B Flat Minor Sonata*. The style is always extremely personal and easily recognizable as Chopin. The communication with the listener is always simple and direct—there is no heavy overlay of philosophy or drama. Perhaps the preoccupation with short forms demands this directness for there is no room for a mood to develop. The mood is immediate, intensifying and subsiding, and in some of the longer works changing, but for the most part, the music makes the listener instantly privy to the innermost feelings of the composer.

Hector Berlioz (1803–1869)

Berlioz was the son of a country doctor who expected his son to follow in his footsteps. The young Berlioz did earn a Bachelor of Science degree from the Medical School in Paris. But from the very beginning his first interest was music. Receiving little encouragement from his father, he nevertheless taught himself to sing at sight and to play the flute and the guitar. A book on harmony started him composing, and at the age of fifteen, with a kind of brash assurance that was frequently to manifest itself throughout his life, he sent his first works to one of the foremost Paris publishers—a vain but valiant effort. He composed an opera and a Mass and reached the age of twenty-three before he finally became a student at the *Conservatoire* where he received formal training in harmony, counterpoint and composition. He supported himself for a while as a singer in the choruses of a theatre and during this period fell in love with an Irish actress, Henrietta Smithson, who rejected him. Always dramatic in his reactions, the rejection produced one of his most remarkable works—an autobiographical *Episode de la Vie d'un Artiste* (*Episode in the Life of an Artist*), better known as the *Symphonie Fantastique*, which follows an artist's vision of his beloved through his early reveries and passions, his romantic dreams of a grand ball and of scenes in the country, and then, in the pain and bitterness of rejection, his vivid imaginings of a march to the scaffold and a witches' sabbath. Throughout the five movements of the work the theme of the beloved appears in varied forms as a unifying motive or an *"idée fixe"* (fixed idea). This programmatic symphony is an astonishing work, especially from a young man of twenty-six with only minimal musical training. One wonders if he would ever have written such a work had his musical education been more extensive and formal. His handling of the orchestra is daringly innovative especially in the writing for the percussion which he uses with what must have seemed like reckless abandon only three years after Beethoven's death. The English horn, French horn, viola, and lower brass play as no one before had ever directed them. Symphonic form gives way to programmatic urgency (the demands of the story). Melody and harmony take on a freedom, almost a wildness, that academic training could never have produced. In short, he produced a work that was literally decades ahead of his time. Franz Liszt was tremendously impressed with it and with Berlioz and did much to further the young man's career.

At the same time, Berlioz won the *Grand Prix de Rome* (this was his fifth try for the prize), not with the *Symphonie Fantastique*, but rather with a cantata, *Sardanapale*, a much more conventional work which is never performed.

Some years later, he renewed his pursuit of Henrietta Smithson and married her. It was not a happy marriage, but they did have a son, Louis. A second marriage after Henrietta's death was not very happy either. Nor did he earn much from his music. Since he didn't play the piano, he was denied a post as teacher of harmony at the *Conservatoire*. He was later appointed librarian. And because he was no virtuoso, he was in demand mostly as conductor of his own works. But since his works required large orchestras with extra instrumentation, sometimes two and three times the normal number of players, there weren't too many opportunities for such appearances. He did, however, make several concert tours which were always much more successful in Russia, Germany, England than in France. He took to writing criticism, which he did brilliantly. He also wrote an excellent *Treatise on Orchestration*, still a very respected book.

His greatest disappointments came in the area of his most ambitious works, his operas. He wrote three operas: *Benvenuto Cellini, Les Troyens* and *Beatrice and Benedict,* a forgotten monodrama called *Lelio* and a dramatic cantata which has been staged as an opera called *The Damnation of Faust.* Of these, only *Beatrice and Benedict* achieved a moderate success. *Les Troyens* (*The Trojans*) was so long it had to be divided into two operas, only one of which was produced during Berlioz's lifetime. He wrote a *Requiem* on commission from the French government and was honored with membership in the Institute.

Today his dramatic symphony, *Romeo et Juliette,* the *Symphonie Fantastique, Harold in Italy* (a symphony with viola obligatto), the *Roman Carnival Overture,* the *Requiem,* an oratorio *L'Enfance du Christ* are performed frequently and at least two of the operatic works, the *Damnation of Faust* and *Les Troyens,* have excited interest in the major opera houses of the world. Berlioz was a rebel and a romantic, given to excess and exaggeration and lacking in the discipline of thorough training, but he was also a true "original" with the stamp of genius.

THE LATE ROMANTIC PERIOD

In the second half of the nineteenth century, Romanticism grew into a tree of many branches, some entangled in competitive struggle, and some blooming tranquilly side by side. The program music Beethoven had experimented with and that Berlioz had produced so vigorously, was taken up by Liszt and Strauss and many others. On the other hand, the more formal aspects that Beethoven had so enriched and enlarged became the inspiration for Brahms. Opera trod new paths with Verdi, Wagner and Puccini and music in general, as we have already said, reflected national histories and cultures. But the romantic emotional exuberance, the lyrical melodic sweeps, the rhythmic and harmonic freedom and the endless exploration of orchestral possibilities and expansions that characterized the first half of the nineteenth century continued unabated.

Johannes Brahms (1833–1897)

Brahms rounds off "the three B's" (Bach, Beethoven and Brahms) and his *First Symphony* is sometimes referred to as Beethoven's Tenth, all of which helps us to place him in the Classic tradition. It is true that, except for his songs and choral works, his music is pure or absolute with no programmatic connotations. His forms are, for the most part, traditional, but expanded and masterfully intricate. However, his melodies are lyrical and long, his rhythms varied and involved, his orchestra big, his emotional range reaches from the intimate to the universal and from the delicate to the tempestuous; all this is in the Romantic tradition. In Brahms the two traditions seem to coexist and produce some of the nineteenth century's greatest music. But during his lifetime, he was often the center of critical controversy. Berlioz, Liszt and Wagner became the champions of "the music of the future," and although Liszt tried hard to win Brahms over to his programmatic musical philosophy, Brahms remained steadfastly "pure" and even signed a manifesto declaring his position.

He was born in Hamburg, the son of a double bass player and was given good instruction in music at an early age. The family was poor and the young Brahms worked in theatres, bars and as accompanist. He became the accompanist for Eduard Remenyi, a Hungarian violin virtuoso, who not only introduced him to many musicians, but to Hungarian music which fascinated Brahms and which he later used in his famous *Hungarian Dances*.

His early works, piano sonatas and songs, came to the attention of Robert Schumann who welcomed the young composer into his home and hailed him as a "young eagle" who trod "new paths." Schumann's praise gave Brahms easier access to publishers and served to spread his fame. He did some concertizing, but much preferred a quiet life devoted to composition. Nevertheless, he spent many years moving about Germany and Austria, before finally settling down in Vienna. His native city of Hamburg was more reserved in its acceptance of his music than were some other towns. This bothered him, especially since he was devoted to his birthplace and expected greater recognition from it. It may have been a factor in his choice of Vienna as a home.

His friendship with the Schumann family did not cease with Robert's tragic death. A very strong platonic bond developed between Brahms and Clara Schumann which lasted as long as they lived. Clara frequently performed Brahms' piano works along with those of her husband and did much to popularize them. Brahms never married.

He began writing for the orchestra in his mid-twenties, but his *First Symphony in C Minor* appeared when he was forty-three. It is a forceful and dramatic work, building up mighty tensions in its first and last movements and resolving them in triumphant glory, stopping along the way in the second and third movements for moments of tender lyricism and calm reflection. The *Second Symphony in D Major* is, perhaps, less forceful and more pastoral although its last movement ends in a brilliant blaze. The *Third in F Major* and *Fourth in E Minor* are again more dramatic with the last movement of the *Fourth* generally recognized as one of the greatest examples of the variation form ever written. For his third movements Brahms frequently replaced the minuet or scherzo with a form of his own devising, generally an allegretto not as formal as a minuet nor as dashing as a scherzo, often in duple instead of triple meter.

In addition to his piano music, songs and four great symphonies, Brahms wrote much wonderful chamber music in many varied combinations. His two *Concertos for the Piano* (in D minor and B flat major), the *Violin Concerto in D Major* and the *Double Concerto for Violin and Cello* are constantly played masterpieces. He wrote no operas, but a great deal of choral music, the most famous of which is the *German Requiem* begun originally after his friend Schumann's death and finished after the death of his mother.

He was honored with the honorary degree of Doctor of Philosophy by the University of Breslau and his thanks were expressed in the beautiful *Academic Festival Overture* in which he uses some traditional German student songs and *Gaudeamus Igitur* as themes. His *Variations on a Theme by Haydn* is another impressive orchestral work. It is nice to remember that the man capable of so much profundity, grandeur, and nobility, could also give us the wonderfully gentle and simple song the world will always refer to as *Brahms' Lullaby*.

Franz Liszt (1811–1886)

A supreme virtuoso at the piano, a tireless composer and arranger, a champion and friend of many young composers, and companion of most of the great ones, a man whose strongly religious inclinations eventually made him take minor orders and the title of Abbé but which in no way interfered with an active and sometimes scandalous lovelife, both influential and flamboyant, Franz Liszt emerges as one of the most interesting personalities of the Romantic period. His family on his father's side was Hungarian, of Magyar descent and noble lineage. His father served for many years as steward of the Esterhazy estates in Hungary and knew many of the great musicians who enjoyed the patronage of that family, among them the great Haydn. Franz, at the age of nine, gave a series of astounding concerts that caused the local nobility to send him to Vienna for lessons from the best teacher. His career as a child prodigy continued with great success in London and Paris. His virtuosity increased phenomenally and he was soon recognized as the greatest pianist of his day. Meanwhile he was composing, mostly for the piano, original works that challenged his own technical powers and some flashy but rather skillful transcriptions (piano versions) of the popular operatic and orchestral works of the day including music by Rossini, Donizetti, Weber, Paganini, Bach and Berlioz. About halfway through his life he abandoned his career as a virtuoso and turned his attention more seriously to composition, especially along the lines that Berlioz had explored. In such works as *Les Préludes, Tasso, Mazeppa,* and *Mephisto Waltz* he developed the symphonic poem (or tone poem). Even his two symphonies, the *Faust Symphony* and the *Dante Symphony,* are highly programmatic. But they are loosely structured and frequently repetitious with ideas that are often more pompous than profound and effects that are merely theatrical rather than dramatic. Nevertheless, he became the leader of those composers and musicians who thought they were striving for the "music of the future" and he was very helpful to many of them.

During the early virtuoso period he had been involved with the Countess d'Agoult, a novelist who, like George Sand, wrote under the masculine name, Daniel Stern. Although they never married, they were together for ten increasingly stormy years and had three children, including a daughter, Cosima, who became Wagner's wife.

The following period, at Weimar, was shared with Princess Carolyn Sayn-Wittgenstein who seems to have broadened his horizons both in composition and as an impressario (producer of the works of others). Liszt gave or arranged for the first performances of Wagner's *Tannhauser, Lohengrin* and *Flying Dutchman,* Berlioz's *Benvenuto Cellini* as well as operas by Schubert and Schumann. He befriended Chopin and even the young Brahms who later came to represent just the opposite of Liszt's musical philosophy.

Liszt showed a great interest in Hungarian Gypsy music and composed a whole series of *Hungarian Rhapsodies* for piano, some of which he transcribed for orchestra. There is also a *Hungarian Fantasy* for piano and orchestra. These are very attractive and are based on Gypsy or Magyar melodies or their derivatives. He encouraged other composers to dip into their own national music, notably Dvorak and Grieg.

Among his other works, the best known are: *Les Préludes*, a philosophic symphonic poem that describes life and its struggles as a series of preludes to that great mystery that awaits us in death; two *Piano Concertos*, one in *E flat* and the other in *A*; *Mephisto Waltz* (piano version) and the ever popular *Liebestraum*. He wrote some oratorios and other religious music and some songs, but no operas and no chamber music.

Although Liszt developed the symphonic poem and used the orchestra imaginatively, and his piano music stretched keyboard technique to new and greater limits, the man was greater than his music. He influenced, taught and encouraged so many musicians, so generously and unselfishly that he must be considered a great Romanticist even if he is somewhat less than a great composer.

*   *   *

LATE ROMANTIC OPERA

Late Romantic opera is dominated by the enormous genius of Guiseppe Verdi and Richard Wagner whose works still form the major part of the repertory of the world's opera houses. Both men had talents too big to be contained by the operatic forms as they found them. Verdi took these forms and enlarged and refashioned them to suit his purposes. Wagner quickly abandoned them and struck out along entirely new and original paths.

*   *   *

Guiseppe Verdi (1813–1901)

The "grand old man" of Italian opera began life as the son of a poor inkeeper in a tiny town. His musical education was thus rather limited and it was only through the charity of the local townspeople that he was sent to Milan at the age of nineteen to enter the Conservatory. He was denied admission because his piano playing was considered inadequate and he was too old for the entering class. He studied privately, married a home town girl and, at twenty-six, had his first opera produced at La Scala, Milan's great opera house. Within a two year span his two children and his young wife died and his second opera was a failure. Verdi was shattered by all this and was ready to abandon composition, but he became interested in the Biblical story of Nebuchadnezzar, fashioning from it his first great success, the opera *Nabucco*. Verdi, like many of the young Italian artists and intellectuals of that time, was much concerned with Italy's struggle to throw off foreign domination and emerge as an independent and unified nation. His early operas, such as *I Lombardi*, *Ernani* and *Macbeth*, have plots that deal with heroes who oppose tyrants and contain stirring choruses that became rallying songs for Italian patriots. But his more important works belong to the middle of his career. *Rigoletio* is the tragic story of a court jester who tries to protect his beautiful daughter from the corrupt Duke for whom he works. He fails in this and his efforts to revenge himself against the duke result in his daughter's death. *Il Trovatore* is a more complicated story of a revenge that backfires with the hero being executed by his own brother. *La Traviata* is a more realistic tragedy dealing with a father's attempt to break up an idyllic love affair between his son and a woman the father considers "not good enough." These operas all have great arias, choruses, duets, trios, quartets etc. But the "connecting tissues," or recitatives, are in and of themselves highly melodic and well supported by the orchestra which is used throughout in very expressive ways. The effect is a more consistent continuity as contrasted with the stop and go effect of the "aria-recitative-aria" pattern of earlier operas. The melodies are not just beautiful, but carefully matched to the character and situation so that they are dramatically apt. Verdi's sense of theatre was strong and unerring. When, as in the famous *Miserere* scene in *Il Trovatore* he mixes an off-stage chorus of monks intoning the *Miserere* against the imprisoned and about to be executed hero singing of his love for the heroine who alone is visible on the darkened stage and who adds her grief-stricken utterances to the music, the effect is overwhelming and absolutely spellbinding.

Verdi's popularity became so great that he was persuaded to become a member of the new Italian Parliament. However, this was a brief interlude and he soon resumed composing. *Sicilian Vespers, Simon Boccanegra, The Masked Ball, The Force of Destiny* and *Don Carlos* round out the middle period.

But even greater things were yet to come. Verdi was approached to write an opera to be produced in Egypt to celebrate the opening of the Suez Canal. He didn't make the opening, but two years later

The exotic Egyptian setting and pagentry of Aida.

Aida was given its first performance in Egypt. This tale of the ill-fated love of a victorious Egyptian general for a captive Ethiopian princess which leads him inadvertently to treachery and both of them to death, is probably the most popular and most often performed of all operas. The exotic Egyptian setting, the rich and splendid pageantry and a gripping story of passion, jealousy and patriotism call for music that is both colorful and strong. This Verdi supplied on a scale that far surpassed any of his previous successes. He followed *Aida* with a *Requiem* in honor of his friend, the writer and patriot, Manzoni. It is a work more operatic than religious, but awesome in its sincerity and power.

For the next thirteen years Verdi wrote no music, but he met Arrigo Boito, poet and composer, who provided librettos for his last two operas, *Otello* and *Falstaff*. These were produced when Verdi was seventy-four and eighty years old. What makes this remarkable is not only that he was still able to write opera, but that his skill and genius were still increasing. Boito's libretto for the opera *Otello* is one of the most tightly knit, well constructed dramas ever to grace the stage. Many critics find it better theatre than the Shakespeare play that inspired it. And the wonderful Verdi music further illuminates the characters and the action, giving us yet another masterpiece.

The more important treatment of "connecting tissues" or recitative that Verdi began in his earlier works and continued with remarkable results in both *Aida* and *Otello* comes to glorious fruition in *Falstaff*, also based on Shakespeare, where arias and ensembles blend into the musical continuity, never stopping the forward dramatic drive.

Verdi was sometimes accused of copying or imitating Wagnerian techniques (which we will explore next). While it is true that he sometimes identified a theme with a character, and that he gave added significance to the orchestra, especially in recitative passages and in preludes and overtures, he always considered the voices first. Throughout its history opera has frequently been called a singer's art. Composers too often acceded to singers' demands for special arias or more florid passages, sometimes in total disregard of the dramatic suitability. With Verdi it became a vocal art. He understood and wrote with consummate skill for the voice, but he never forgot that he was writing for the theatre and in the theatre "the play's the thing." He died at the age of eighty-eight leaving the bulk of his estate for the support of a shelter he established for less fortunate musicians.

Richard Wagner (1813–1883)

Wagner at first wanted to be a poet and writer although he became interested in music in his early teens. He started the study of piano when he was eleven and wrote a poetic play when he was fourteen. Upon hearing Beethoven's music for Goethe's play, *Egmont*, he decided his play should have music too and he began to try to compose.

He studied violin and theory, arranged Beethoven's *Ninth Symphony* for piano, and composed an unsuccessful *Overture in B flat*, before he began serious music study at the age of eighteen. From the very beginning he wrote his own librettos for his operas or music-dramas as he called them. He also wrote voluminously on all manner of subjects such as "Art and Religion," "The Art of the Future," "Art and Revolution," "Opera and Drama," "On German Music," "On Conducting," and "Judaism in Music." He carried on an extensive correspondence, and over a period of fifteen years wrote a very long and detailed autobiography called *Mein Leben* (*My Life*). He can hardly be accused of having neglected his literary inclinations. His earliest operas were not successful, but *Rienzi* and *The Flying Dutchman* were. In *Rienzi* Wagner still follows the model of earlier composers or successful contemporaries such as Meyerbeer. However, with *The Flying Dutchman* he begins to find his own way and create his own style. Inspired by a rough voyage Wagner had undertaken from Riga to London, *The Flying Dutchman* tells of the legendary sea captain who must sail the seas forever unless released from this curse by the love of a pure and faithful woman. He is allowed only a brief time once every seven years to search for her. Such a story shows the influence of von Weber, for it is a folk tale with strong romantic overtones of magic and mystery. But the very first notes of the *Overture* establish a unique style of strength, a sureness of instrumental coloration and a harmonic sophistication that is the mark of Wagner. To be sure, there are still set arias and choruses, but they are part of a fascinating symphonic web that Wagner weaves with the orchestra. Already he is using musical themes or *leitmotifs* to represent characters or situations. This was not original with Wagner. Berlioz had used the *idée fixe* in the *Fantastic Symphony*. But Wagner was a master contrapuntalist, and the intertwining he achieves with these *motifs* is not only superb music, but very often a musical delineation of the intricacies of plot and motivation. *Tannhäuser* and *Lohengrin* followed next. The former deals with sacred and profane love and involves a song contest. The latter deals with love, chivalry and witchcraft. Both move further along in orchestral integration, but still retain many big operatic moments in fairly traditional style. The *Pilgrims' Chorus* from *Tannhäuser* and the *Wed-*

131

ding March from *Lohengrin* are universally popular examples of such moments.

Legend and history combine in Wagner to produce a strong Germanic style that emphasizes the heroic. This is especially evident in the *Der Ring des Nibelungen,* a series of four music-dramas on which he worked, intermittently, for about twenty-six years. The four operas—*Das Rheingold, Die Walküre, Siegfried, Götterdämmerung,* tell a very complicated tale of a struggle for power between the old gods of Norse mythology and the *Nibelungen* (dwellers of the under world). Giants, dwarfs, dragons as well as mortals are involved and much is made of the supernatural. All the human emotions are explored. The hero, Siegfried, appearing in the last two operas, is a mortal almost godlike in his strength and lack of fear. The heroine, Brunhilde, appearing in all but the first opera, is a goddess made mortal by her human sympathies and her ability to love. But even love falls victim to treachery and the lust for power, and Siegfried, Brunhilde, and the gods themselves all perish in *Götterdämmerung (Twilight of the Gods).* The four operas are welded together not only by the continuing story line and the many characters that appear in two or more of them, but also by the many *leitmotifs* that represent these characters and serve to guide the listener through the long and busy plot. Wagner's incredible skill in combining and modifying these *motifs* lifts the orchestra to an importance and to a size and grandeur it had never before achieved in opera. Writing his own librettos, Wagner felt his drama and his music must form a perfect unity. More and more he avoided the big aria or the showy quartet. Instead the words and music flow in a long continuing line, broken only by changes in the action and never by a desire to show a tenor or soprano off to best advantage. So exacting was Wagner regarding the proper performances of his music-dramas, that a special theatre was built to his specifications at Bayreuth in Germany, where he could supervise every phase of the production, even costumes and scenery. Wagner festivals are still given there annually.

Wagner's ideas about opera stirred up considerable reaction and one of the most prominent Viennese critics, Hanslick, who had praised Brahms, was strongly anti-Wagner. With his only comic

music-drama, *Die Meistersinger von Nürnberg,* Wagner took his revenge. In this story of how a young man wins the hand of the girl
he loves in a song contest, the strict rules of the medieval guilds are
confronted with the ardor and sincerity of youthful love. One of the
guild members, Beckmesser, insists on all the rules. He cannot
tolerate anything new or different or creative. Of course, Beckmesser
is a thinly disguised Hanslick and in the course of the opera he is
made to look ridiculous.

Wagner was not an easy or ingratiating personality. Self-centered,
demanding and extremely egotistical, he made enemies easily and
often sorely tried his friends. He eloped with Cosima von Bulow, the
wife of his good friend, Hans von Bulow, and the daughter of Liszt.
He and Cosima had three children before her marriage to von Bulow
was annulled and they were able to marry. Wagner's first wife,
Minna, had been patient and long suffering. They had separated
several times over his "affairs" but she died before the elopement.

It is fitting, therefore, that a man whose own experience of love
was vivid and hardly conventional should write one of the greatest
works of love music, *Tristan und Isolde.* Again, a medieval story, it
tells of the knight, Tristan, sent by King Mark to fetch the Princess
Isolde to be the King's bride. Isolde is unwilling and attempts to
poison Tristan but her maid substitutes a love potion and the two
fall hopelessly in love. The power of the potion forces them to betray
the King, but not until they sing some of the most passionate and
ecstatic love music ever written.

Wagner's last music-drama was *Parsifal,* a story about the Holy
Grail and the forces of good and evil, of innocence and temptation.
And here his religious intensity matches the passion and powerful
heroics of his previous works.

Wagner's music-dramas present us with symphonic orchestral development, integrated with vocal lines into a total texture. The voice
no longer predominates as in most Italian and French operas. The
operas require concentration and a good memory for recognizing
the *leitmotifs.* But they more than repay the effort, for they contain
many moments of the most exciting and exalted music.

*   *   *

Toward the end of the Romantic period opera took a turn away from the heroic and legendary. It began to concern itself with ordinary people in a more commonplace world. Mascagni's *Cavalleria Rusticana* deals with love, jealousy and violence among Italian peasants. So does Leoncavallo's *I Pagliacci*, which adds the color of a strolling band of players and some backstage intrigue to the local scene. Puccini's *La Bohème* deals with life among the struggling young artists, writers and musicians of Paris. *Tosca* treats of love, espionage and police matters. This realism or *verismo* exerted some influence on opera in the twentieth century, but many composers, especially among the French, continued dealing with subjects of more epic or romantic nature such as Gounod's *Faust* and Massenet's *Manon*. The Russians looked into their own history for subjects. And even Puccini's later works returned to exotic subjects as in *Madame Butterfly* (Japanese) and *Turandot* (ancient Chinese). However Puccini did give us an opera about our American Gold Rush, *The Girl of the Golden West*, which, despite its Western saloon setting, still sounds very Italian! (Mascagni 1863–1945, Leoncavallo 1858–1919, Puccini 1858–1924)

Peter Ilyich Tchaikovsky (1840–1893)

Tchaikovsky is one of the most often performed composers although serious musicians tend to consider him "too popular." His music is frequently very sentimental, often bombastic and sometimes merely pretty or trivial. Yet few composers speak so directly to the listener with melodies of such surpassing and haunting beauty, or carry him along on a cresting tidal wave of passionate, exhilarating, almost hysterical orchestral climax only to plunge him, seconds later, into the deepest pools of utter despair and profoundest grief. An extremely sensitive man, he wore his heart on his musical sleeve all his life.

Like Schumann, he studied law to please his family, but turned to serious study of music in his early twenties. Devoted to his own family, mother, brothers and sister, he related poorly to women, and a disastrous and very brief marriage resulted in a serious nervous breakdown for him and a suicide attempt and total breakdown for the girl. However, a wealthy woman, Nadejda von Meck, much taken with his music, settled an allowance on him with the stipulation that they never meet. This relieved him of financial worry and of the necessity of teaching, so that he was able to devote all his time to composition. The arrangement continued for a number of years and resulted not only in much wonderful music but a fascinating correspondence in which Tchaikovsky gives intimate glimpses into his feelings, especially as they relate to and affect his compositions. When the correspondence (and the allowance) were finally terminated by Madame von Meck with no explanation, Tchaikovsky was much hurt and depressed by the loss of this "beloved friend" whom he had never met, although by this time he was world famous and had no need of her financial help.

Tchaikovsky wrote eleven operas, two of which still figure in the international repertoire. They are *Eugene Onegin* and *Pique Dame* and both deal with tragic love affairs. He composed three ballets which are still the most popular full-length ballets ever written (A full-length ballet occupies an entire evening in the theatre—as opposed to a varied program of short ballets.) *Swan Lake* is a tragedy while *The Sleeping Beauty* and *The Magic Nutcracker* end happily. All three are fairy tales and contain some very charming music.

Of his six symphonies, the last three appear constantly on concert programs, as do his first *Piano Concerto in Bb Minor*, the *Violin Concerto in D Major* and the *Capriccio Italian*. We have already mentioned his concert overture *Romeo and Juliet* (Chapters II and XI).

His chamber music, piano music, some religious choral music, and his songs all reveal the same gift for lovely melody. Among the songs *None But the Lonely Heart* is a real gem.

Tchaikovsky himself claimed that his handling of form was his chief weakness and his fellow Russians criticized him for not being Russian enough. But in the presence of the music itself these criticisms seem petty. Certainly the long works hold together and engage our interest and we come away remembering many of the themes. That is what form is about. And so many of the melodies are so Russian in style and feeling (and often are really Russian folk songs, for example, the main theme of the last movement of the *Fourth Symphony*). He was intensely patriotic. *Marche Slav* and the famous *Overture 1812* in which he describes the Russian defeat of Napoleon are eloquent evidence of this.

His last symphony, the *Pathétique,* runs the extravagant emotional gamut from rage to romance but ends in a slough of despondency. A few days after its first performance Tchaikovsky died of cholera, contracted as a result of drinking contaminated water during an epidemic. Because of the dark mood of this last symphony and his predisposition to melancholic periods, many think he drank the water intentionally.

Richard Strauss (1864–1949)

Although he lived well into the twentieth century, Richard Strauss was really a Romanticist. His father, a horn player, was an anti-Wagnerite and saw to it that his son had a thorough Classical training, but it wasn't long before the young Strauss became a convert to the "music of the future" as developed by Wagner, Liszt and Berlioz. Working chiefly on symphonic poems, operas and songs he produced some very great works. He developed prodigious technique as a composer and this skill is evident in all his work, but the substance of his output varies considerably. With respect to the tone poems, he took the form of Liszt and expanded it, giving it greater specificity and realism. He gives us detailed musical descriptions of specific events such as a horse charging through a medieval marketplace and knocking over cartloads of livestock so that we hear the quacking of ducks and the "oink" of pigs, the sounds being produced by orchestral instruments. Sometimes he carries realism even further and uses a wind machine, like the ones used backstage in theatres, to produce the sound of howling winds. His orchestra is large in the Wagnerian sense and he uses themes to represent characters and ideas in much the same way. He weaves these themes into a complicated contrapuntal texture and orchestrates with a sense of tone color that is always vivid, sometimes magical and peculiarly his own. His best works in this form are *Don Juan, Thus Spake Zarathustra, Death and Transfiguration* and the ever popular masterpiece *Till Eulenspiegel's Merry Pranks.* His *Ein Heldenleben* (A Hero's Life) and *Domestic Symphony* are rather egotistical autobiographical works that do not hold audience interest as well as the others.

In opera he is best known for *Der Rosenkavalier, Salome, Elektra* and *Ariadne auf Naxos,* all in very different styles. *Der Rosenkavalier* is a lush romantic love story with comic overtones and lovely lyric music flavored throughout with Viennese waltzes. *Salome* tells the Biblical story of the jaded princess who demands the head of John the Baptist as her price for dancing for King Herod and is a work that combines a more stark idiom with the lushness. *Elektra* is based on the great Greek legend in which Orestes, urged on by his sister, Elektra, avenges the murder of their father, Agamemnon, by killing their mother, Clytemnestra, and her lover, Aegisthus. Here Strauss builds suspense, horror and terror with a dissonance and jagged angularity that point the way to much later twentieth century developments. *Ariadne,* a silly mixture of Greek legend, a Molière play and Italian *Commedia dell'Arte,* is again in more conservative style but, despite some lovely moments, fails to measure up to *Der Rosenkavalier.*

While his output is uneven, Strauss at his best is masterful, especially with respect to orchestral coloration, evocation of mood, and apt musical description of events or characters.

* * *

Two late Romantic composers who were influenced by the big orchestra, the large dimensions and thematic intricacies of the Wagnerian style, were Anton Bruckner (1824–1896) and Gustave Mahler (1860–1911). Both were primarily symphonists, but even more Romantic than Brahms. Of the two, Mahler was the more original, innovative and profound, often employing solo voices and choruses in symphonic works. Both men were deeply religious, Bruckner in the more literal sense and Mahler more mystically; these traits are evident in their work.

Camille Saint-Saëns (1835–1921)

Saint-Saëns is a French composer of the late nineteenth century— a Romanticist with Classical leanings. But in addition to symphonies, concertos and chamber music he also wrote symphonic poems in the manner of Liszt and Berlioz, the best known of these being the *Danse Macabre* and the *Spinning Wheel of Omphale.* His opera, *Samson and Delilah,* is a world favorite, as is each of the following: the *Third Symphony* (with Organ), the *Piano Concerto in G Minor,* the *Introduction and Rondo Capriccioso,* for violin and orchestra, the *Cello Concerto in A Minor* and, of course, *The Swan* from the *Carnival of Animals.* Rarely universal or deep, he was nevertheless always highly melodic and elegant and often very colorful and exciting.

César Franck (1822–1890)

Born in Belgium, Franck received the major part of his musical education in Paris and worked there for most of his life, chiefly as organist and choirmaster at the church of St. Clothilde, but also as professor of organ at the *Conservatoire.* A Romanticist with a strong mystical and religious bent, he nevertheless wrote some of his most important works in abstract forms. He had a way of combining essentially simple but beautiful melodies with very sophisticated and complex harmonies. His *Symphony in D Minor* is a great work in cyclical form (see this chapter, section on Beethoven). The *Symphonic Variations* for piano and orchestra is another. The *Sonata for Violin and Piano* is much performed and the lovely *Panis Angelicus* is a short example of his considerable output of church music. Symphonic poems, much organ and piano music complete the list.

Sergei Rachmaninov (1873–1943)

A Russian virtuoso pianist who permanently left his native land in 1917, Rachmaninov did most of his composing before that date and so really belongs to the nineteenth century. Much influenced by Tchaikovskian Romanticism, Rachmaninov wrote extremely long, expressive melodies and supported them with rich harmonies and colorful instrumentation. His *Piano Concerto #2 in C Minor* is among the most popular works in that form and is filled with gorgeous melodies, one frequently borrowed for popular music. The *Second Symphony* and the *Variations on a Theme by Paganini* are important and beautiful works. (The latter, composed in 1934, is one of the few "late works".) Among his many piano pieces, the *Prelude in C Sharp Minor* is known to every student of the piano.

THE NATIONALISTS

Music often achieves a nationalistic flavor or effect unintentionally as in Verdi's early operas, where the choruses and plots fell right in line with the ideals of an Italy struggling to be free of foreign domination. But in the second half of the nineteenth century many composers became aware of their roots and strove consciously to give musical expression to these ideas. They used folk songs as important themes and they structured their works around national legends and history. They featured characteristic instruments and tone colors and idiomatic harmonies and rhythms, as Chopin did in his *Mazurkas* and *Polonaises*.

Nowhere is this conscious nationalism more apparent than in Russian music of the nineteenth century. Russia's unique Orthodox church music and the many different types of folk music of the varied groups of peasants that people that huge nation offer the composer endless material. However, Russian aristocracy, beginning with Peter, the Great in the seventeenth century, looked westward for cultural development and tended to copy French, German and Italian models. And even in the nineteenth century when Mikhail Glinka (1804–1857) and Alexander Dargomijsky (1813–1869) had already turned their attention to creating a truly Russian music, Tchaikovsky and Rubinstein were accused of being too much under the influence of German music. Glinka had exerted a great influence on Mily Balakirev (1837–1910) who then proceeded to gather round himself a group of young musical amateurs with the avowed purpose of developing a nationalistic Russian music. These included César Cui (1835–1918), Modest Mussorgsky (1839–1881), Alexander Borodin (1833–1887), and Nikolai Rimsky-Korsakov (1844–1908). The Russian Five, as Balakirev and his disciples are sometimes called, had one thing in common. They all lacked any great degree of formal musical education either as performers or composers, having generally been trained for other careers. Cui was trained as a military engineer and later taught engineering at the Military Academy, devoting his spare time to composing and more importantly to writing articles and criticism calling attention to the work of the others in the group. Borodin was a doctor who taught chemistry at the Medical School and whose research in medical chemistry was distinguished enough to have earned him renown even if he had never composed the opera *Prince Igor*, the tone poem *On the Steppes of Central Asia*, a popular *Second Symphony* and a lovely *String Quartet*. He called himself a "Sunday composer."

The most talented and original of the Five was Modeste Mussorgsky, who also was trained for a military career, but who abandoned it to devote himself full time to music. Learning his trade as he went along, he produced among other works two great operas, *Boris Godunov* (an overwhelming masterpiece) and *Khovantshina* (both operas based on Russian history), the tone poem *Night on Bald Mountain*, the ever popular *Pictures at an Exhibition* (composed originally for the piano—later orchestrated by several composers), and a number of wonderful songs. Mussorgsky, perhaps because he had little formal training, was harmonically daring, using the raw materials of folk music without over-refining them. Unfortunately he left many works unfinished and often he submitted them to his friends for criticism. The result was that much of his work has come down to us in edited versions which have much of their original strength "edited" out of them. Only recently has the Russian government shown an interest in going back to original manuscripts so that Mussorgsky's music (and Borodin's too) can be presented as it was originally written.

Nicolai Rimsky-Korsakov, the youngest of the Five, has achieved the greatest popularity with such works as *Scheherezade* (described in Chapter VIII on Program Music), the *Russian Easter Overture* (based on church themes, but wildly colorful in orchestration), the *Capriccio Espagnol*, the *Antar Symphony*, two of his many operas, *Sadko and Le Coq d'Or* (*The Golden Cockerel*), and the short but world famous *Flight of the Bumblebee*. He was trained as a naval officer, served on a three year cruise which brought him to New York, and on returning to Russia continued in secretarial naval service and as Inspector of Naval Bands for some time. He was appointed Professor of Practical Composition and Instrumentation at the St. Petersburg Conservatory although, as he himself said, he knew so little of form, harmony, counterpoint and orchestration that he had to study to keep a step ahead of the class. And study he did, so that he produced a text in harmony and another on *Principles of Orchestration* which is still much used. It was Rimsky-Korsakov who did most of the completing and editing of Mussorgsky's and of Borodin's unfinished work. He did this with the best intentions of perpetuating their music, not realizing how much he was imposing of his own style and ideas. However, he was also a great teacher, numbering Prokofiev and Stravinsky among his students.

Balakirev, who inspired the group, is known in this country only for a tone poem, *Islamey*, written originally for piano, then orchestrated. He did much to bring about first performances of the works of the others, but he proved too domineering a leader and as each of the Five matured he had less influence on them.

It is interesting to note that in their antipathy to "Western" and particularly German influences over Russian music, they so frequently looked "eastward" for inspiration, drawing heavily on the Oriental and Moslem strains in Russian history. *Islamey, Scheherezade, Prince Igor, Steppes of Central Asia, Coq d'Or* are just a few examples of this Eastern influence. But "Mother Russia" was not neglected in such works as *Boris Godunov* and *Khovantshina* with their Moscow settings and in the *Russian Easter Overture* with its vivid evocation of Russian cathedral splendor.

*　　*　　*

Bohemia, or what we now call Czechoslovakia, like Italy, was plagued for centuries by foreign rule. Prague saw the premier of several of Mozart's operas and was host to many Austrian, Italian and German musicians. Bedřich Smetana (1824–1884) was one of the leaders in asserting the strong individuality of Czech or Bohemian culture and especially music. His comic opera, *The Bartered*

Bride, filled with village-type songs and dances, is universally popular. His cycle of symphonic poems, *Ma Vlast* (*My Country*), contains the *Moldau,* a description of a river as it begins at its source in two mountain springs that join to form a stream that runs through forests and rural glades, gathering force until it makes its turbulent way over rapids to flow majestically past ancient Czech fortresses and through the city of Prague.

Antonin Dvorak (1841–1904), following in Smetana's footsteps, wrote operas and symphonic poems, but was much drawn to more abstract works in large forms—symphonies and chamber music, as well as religious works. His melodic, harmonic, and rhythmic styles were strongly colored by his native folk idioms, which he honored with two sets of thoroughly charming *Slavonic Dances* in versions for piano duet and for orchestra. His most famous work, the *New World Symphony* (in E minor), composed while teaching in New York for a two year period during which he was terribly home-sick, displays themes influenced by American Negro spiritual and American Indian melodies which fascinated Dvorak. But so strong was the pull of his native land that many passages in his American symphony come through with a distinct Bohemian flavor. The *Carnaval Overture* is full of the excitement of a country fair and the *Cello Concerto in B Minor,* while somewhat more restrained and sophisticated, is full of glorious melodies with a real peasant dance opening the last movement. The *Humoresque,* a short piano piece, is one of the most popular melodies ever written.

Edvard Grieg (1843–1907)

Grieg is sometimes called the "Chopin of the North" but while the two composers had much in common and Grieg loved Chopin's work, the title does not give us an altogether accurate picture. Both composers wrote much piano music, Chopin almost exclusively, but Grieg wrote some fine instrumental music and some exceptionally wonderful songs as well. Both were daring harmonists, given to reckless changes of key and involved chord structure, but whereas in Chopin this lent a high degree of polish and sophistication to his work, in Grieg one senses an underlying folklike simplicity whose natural boldness and strength finds expression in these chords. Both composers wrote mostly in small forms and yet were able to encompass the widest emotional range. But Chopin favored the abstract, whereas Grieg gave most of his short pieces descriptive names. Chopin's nationalism was expressed in his *Mazurkas* and *Polonaises* and some heroic pieces. Grieg's more intentional nationalism gave rise to the beautiful *Norwegian Dances, Northern Dances and Folk Tunes* and many *Lyric Pieces* (similar to Mendelssohn's *Songs Without Words*) with titles that allude to the Norwegian countryside or to Norwegian legends. Few composers have matched Grieg's ability to catch in music cool, clear mountain landscapes, lonesome lakes and fjords, gentle rolling meadows and farms, rustic villages and peasant vigor.

Best known among his larger works is the incidental music he wrote for Ibsen's folk-play *Peer Gynt*. The music has been gathered into two orchestral suites and is performed far more often than the play that brought it into being. Especially popular is the marvelous *Piano Concerto in A Minor* containing themes that range from the heroic to the pastoral and from the elfin to the passionate. His *Piano Sonata in E Minor* and the *Violin Sonata in C Minor* are ingratiating works. The song *I Love Thee* is one of the most beguiling of all love songs. *Two Elegiac Melodies*, for string orchestra (*Heart Wounds* and *The Last Spring*), are the essence of tender sadness. And all these works bear a melodic and harmonic stamp that is recognizably Grieg's.

Like Chopin, Grieg suffered severe respiratory problems which he felt prevented him from undertaking more ambitious works in larger forms like opera and symphony. But he lived to be sixty-four, gaining great recognition not only in Norway but all over the world, receiving honorary degrees from Cambridge and Oxford and the French Legion of Honor.

Jean Sibelius (1865–1957)

What Grieg is to Norway, Sibelius is to Finland. He, too, loved his native land and especially those aspects of nature most characteristic of it. More remote from central Europe than the rest of

Scandinavia and long under the yoke of Sweden and Imperial Russia, Finland in many respects remained somewhat more primitive than its northern neighbors. Sibelius, himself an introspective and somber personality, admirably projects much of the mystery and remoteness of his country. Using the legends of the *Kalavala*, Finland's national epic poem, Sibelius has given us a series of tone poems dealing with the heroes of ancient Finland and the struggle between paganism and Christianity. *The Swan of Tuoniela, Pohjola's Daughter, The Return of Lemminkäinen* are some of these. Even better known is *Finlandia*, a patriotic outpouring in defiance of Russian control. All these works evoke the vast forests, the brooding, shadowy lakes that reflect them and the lowering northern skies. The mood is generally darker and bolder than Grieg's and developed at greater length.

His major works are his symphonies, of which the *First, Second* and *Fifth* are much played. They show a little of the influence of Tchaikovsky, but they bear the stamp of Sibelius' unique style. The *Violin Concerto* and the *Fourth Symphony* are his most original and most performed works and his *Seventh Symphony* compresses symphonic form into one large movement. The *Valse Triste*, composed as incidental music to a dream-death scene in the drama *Kuolema*, is a shorter work that has become very popular. But it is as a symphonist and in large scale works that Sibelius shines.

*　　*　　*

Spanish music has become identified with a very special and easily recognizable ethnic or national character stemming mainly from two major sources: the *flamenco* or Gypsy influences with their Semitic-Oriental flavors—a result of the long period of Moorish occupation in Spain, and the many special dance rhythms like the *jota, fandango, bolero, tango*—some of these deriving from Spanish commerce with the Americas ("Indies") and Africa. Many non-Spanish composers have been intrigued by these exotic elements and have given us a great deal of "Spanish" music. Debussy's *Iberia*, Rimsky-Korsakov's *Capriccio Espagnole*, Bizet's opera *Carmen* are prime examples. Even native Spanish composers tend to emphasize these elements to the exclusion of other important influences such as the church and its music which had a very pronounced effect in this very Catholic country. The best known Spanish nationalists are Isaac Albéniz (1860–1909), Enrique Granados (1867–1916) and Manuel de Falla (1876–1946). All three wrote many short "Spanish" pieces for piano or voice as well as operas. Albéniz is remembered for the lovely *Tango in D, Cadiz, Cordoba, Seguidillas, Triana* and *Fête-Dieu à Seville,* while Granados also contributed many Spanish dances and songs including a piano collection inspired by the "Maja" paintings of Goya which he later expanded into an opera, *Goyescas.* By far the most sophisticated of the three was de Falla who understood how to write for orchestra better than his compatriots and who, living as he did into the twentieth century, mixed his Spanish nationalism with some impressionistic techniques learned from Debussy and Ravel whose work we have yet to explore. His opera *La Vida Breve,* his ballet *El Amor Brujo* (containing the famous *Ritual Fire Dance*) and *The Three Cornered Hat,* and his imaginative *Nights in the Gardens of Spain* for piano and orchestra are works of size and significance. But the abstractions and profundities of the symphony and the more traditional large forms seemed to hold little attraction for the Spanish Romanticists.

XIV

TWENTIETH CENTURY MUSIC

The twentieth century, like its predecessors, has seen many changes in art, literature and music as well as in every phase of living, but in no previous century has the rate of change been so rapid and the impact so great. Our technological advances, of course, are the reason for this, especially in the area of communication. In earlier days travel was slow, there were no telephones, mail when and where available was expensive and risky, and private messengers were common. Imagine a world with no newspapers and no photography and no recordings or tapes. In such a world it took years for the technique of oil painting which was developing in the Low Countries to reach Italy, and great musicians in one country or even one town could go through an entire career more or less unaware of what great musicians in another town or country were doing. Each of the centuries we have so far studied saw gradual improvement over its predecessor in the communication gap or lag and, with the improvement, a wider dissemination of works of art, literature and music. Today we have instant and mass communication no longer dependent only on the printed or sounded word, but supported by all the vivid world of sight. An art dealer discovers a tribal mask still used by a primitive people in a remote continent and, in a flash, it is seen as a news item on television. A few days later copies of it are available for purchase in smart shops all over the world, and soon it is hanging on the wall of many a home.

Similarly, an important composer prepares a new work for a premiere performance by a major symphony orchestra. The performance is broadcast (or televised) on a nation-wide or even a world-wide network. It is reviewed by the major music critics in the city in which the premiere takes place. But it is also reviewed by the radio, T.V., and music critics of every area in which it was carried by the network. It is then recorded to be sold all over the world. If the work is innovative it can immediately be imitated on a wide scale, and very soon the innovations become trite and "old hat." This puts tremendous pressure on the composer (or any artist, for that matter) to come up continually with something new. Few are the creative artists who can resist this pressure and take the time to nurture and develop an original, individual and consistently maturing style. Too many become experimenters, always trying something novel. And again our ever expanding technology makes this a very easy and attractive path to follow. There are so many new things! In the visual arts, the whole world of plastics and other synthetic materials along with our increased understanding of light and color have intrigued many artists. Even our increased scientific knowledge of time-space relationships is grist for the artist's mill and we find paintings in which profile, full face and three quarter-views of the same subject are superimposed one upon the other since all three views exist at the same time. Thus we get "portraits" with more than the usual number of noses, eyes, ears, etc. or rooms and buildings rendered in multi and simultaneous perspective.

In the language arts, explorations of the psychology of speech, of linguistics, of word symbols and word sounds (not to mention the whole panorama of human experience as reviewed and reinterpreted by the psychologists, scientists and philosophers of the late nineteenth century—and then further analyzed by those of the twentieth century in the light of two devastating World Wars) has led us into many new ways of putting words together. Think, for example, of the works of Gertrude Stein, James Joyce, e.e. cummings, to mention only a few pioneers.

In music, the major scientific advance has been in recording and electronics, but many other avenues of experimentation have been explored, some as the expected outgrowth of nineteenth century developments, others as radical departures and still others as reaction to the radical changes.

*　　*　　*

Beginning with Chopin and Berlioz and furthered by such composers as Wagner and Franck, the increasing use of chromaticism (the introduction of notes, both melodically and harmonically, not in the scale or key of the composition) and of modulation (the

147

changing of key—see Chapter II—section on harmony) began to erode the traditional scale patterns and the whole concept of key feeling (tonality). In much the same way that French painters of the late nineteenth century began to abandon sharp outline drawing in favor of "suggesting" outline by the juxtaposition of color (the edge of a barn in a meadow is where the brown begins and the green stops), so musicians began to break away from the confines of scale and key. Similarly the realism or specificity of musical description that characterized some of the works of Richard Strauss was supplanted by a vague sketch more evocative of mood than picture. This "impressionism" found its most important exponent in Claude Debussy (1862–1918). Paralleling the ideas of the impressionist painters and the symbolist poets, Debussy concerned himself with the mystical, the exotic and with nature. The vague and dreamy style of his *Prelude to the Afternoon of a Faun* has already been described in Chapter VIII on program music. Debussy achieved his effects by extremely original, skillful and delicate orchestration. He wrote in ancient "modes" (the scales of the music of the early Christian Church derived from earlier Greek "modes") and a whole-tone scale in addition to the more usual major and minor scales. He used parallel harmonies generally avoided in the Classic and Romantic periods but much used in early church music (and now in modern music). All this lends an air of antiquity to his *Prelude*. The exotic harmonies, the muted strings, the fascinating melodic interchange of woodwinds and horn makes the music irresistibly sensuous. In a set of *Nocturnes,* Debussy turns his attention to *Nuages* (*Clouds*) and evokes the mood inspired when one watches the slowly everchanging but always same procession of fleecy-white cotton puffs across blue sky. In the same set, *Fêtes* (*Festivals*) recreates the wild abandon of street crowds on a big holiday, building from expectant hush to high hysteria. In *Iberia,* one of a group of orchestral pieces called *Images,* Debussy, who had spent only one day in Spain near the French border, was able, according to the great Spanish composer de Falla, to catch "the intoxicating spell of Andalusian nights." (Almost all of Spain lies between the French border and Andalusia!) It is equally surprising that his greatest orchestral work should be *La Mer* (*The Sea*) when his longest voyage was only a crossing of the English Channel, although he spent much time at the shore. The titles of the three sections of this work summarize the "impressions" which are summoned up. They are *The Sea from Dawn until Noon, Sport of the Waves,* and *Dialogue of the Wind and the Sea.*

Debussy had a special understanding of the piano and wrote works which demanded subtleties of pedaling and tone production that considerably widened the palette (tone-color range) of the instrument. *The Sunken Cathedral, Feux d'artifice (Fire Works), Claire de lune (Moonlight), Two Arabesques, The Girl with Flaxen Hair* are only a few of his miniature pianistic tone poems. *The Children's Corner,* which he wrote for his little daughter contains the famous *Golliwog's Cake Walk* and shows that he was aware of American popular music styles.

Debussy's songs and his opera, *Pelléas et Mélisande,* reveal his unusual gift for using a text so that its musical setting flows as easily as speech while the mood is greatly intensified. He wrote an astonishing *String Quartet* in which the orchestral possibilities of the four instruments are so exploited that a whole new dimension provides contrast to the more conventional intimacy of such a group.

Debussy died of cancer at the age of fifty-six, having created a style so individualistic that he had few successful followers. But he trod several new paths that considerably influenced later developments in twentieth century music. His harmonic freedom and flexibility were another step toward today's atonality (absence of key feeling) and polytonality (music in several keys simultaneously). His rhythms and his form in general also broke down time honored barriers. As for instrumentation, his ability to achieve the maximum effect from a minimum of means marked a significant change from the ever enlarging orchestra of the post-Wagnerians. And while the over-all effect of his "impressionism" on the listener is that of a hazy, soft-focused, brief glance, the score as Debussy wrote it always reveals a remarkable precision and finesse. Nothing is haphazard. Everything emerges just as Debussy had planned. His is a very personal utterance, dealing with the moods and emotions inspired by ideas and images rather than with the realities themselves. As such it is certainly a direct, even an extreme branch of Romanticism, but Debussy's amazing technical daring and originality also make it a germinal part of Modernism if such a name can be applied to the many different aspects of twentieth century music.

Among those who were influenced by Debussy to a greater or lesser degree are Ravel, Dukas, Delius, Vaughan-Williams, de Falla, Scriabin and Griffes.

* * *

Needless to say, in music, as in physics, every action sets up an immediate and opposite reaction. Impressionism inspired such reaction in Eric Satie and a group of French composers known as "*Les Six*" which included Darius Milhaud, Arthur Honegger, Francis Poulenc, Georges Auric, Louis Durey and Germaine Tailleferre. The first three, along with Satie, have achieved more recognition than the others. Their music is frequently bitingly satiric, sometimes realistic (Honegger's *Pacific 231* describes a steam locomotive), strongly dissonant, sometimes revealing the influence of American jazz (Milhaud's *Creation du Monde* [*The Creation of the World*] is an example) and occasionally architectural or formal in the Classic sense. While they seem to have banded together in a spirit of anti-impressionism, they soon went separate ways, exploring many different styles. (Satie 1866–1925, Honegger 1892–1955, Milhaud 1892–1974)

The prefix "neo" is encountered in any treatment of the twentieth century. It means "new," and we have "neo-Romanticism, neo-Classicism, neo-modality, etc. Richard Strauss, Gustave Mahler, Alexander Scriabin and Sergei Rachmaninov were neo-Romantics (especially the first two) in that they took what appealed to them in terms of modern harmony, rhythm and instrumentation and adapted it to their own expressive, essentially Romantic styles.

Since impressionism was itself a form of Romanticism, the neo-Classicists reacted to it as well as to the Romantics. Maurice Ravel (1875–1937), himself considered an impressionist in such works as *La Valse* and *Daphnis et Chloe*, on closer examination proves to be a Classicist who colors and flavors his work with many advanced techniques including the impressionist ones. His chamber music, especially the masterful *Quartet in F*, is almost Mozartian in its clarity and form even though the idiom is unmistakably modern and French. The two works previously mentioned, along with his *Mother Goose Suite*, the *Pavane for a Dead Princess* and the world famous *Bolero* are constantly played. They are more objective (in the Classic manner) than the works of Debussy. They do not overwhelm you with mood and atmosphere. Instead you stand by and watch a great artist at work, admiring how the parts fit together to create a superb and beautifully crafted totality.

Sergei Prokofiev (1891–1953), famous for his charming orchestral fairy tale for children, *Peter and the Wolf*, was another neo-Classicist who peppered his concertos, symphonies, piano and chamber music with intentionally bizarre and humorous effects, introducing a wild and unexpected dissonance or leading a pretty and fairly traditional melody into an awkward and unanticipated skip. Nevertheless, his *Classical Symphony* (scored for Mozartian orchestra) and his *Third Piano Concerto* are most attractive. Along with much music in Classic form (symphonies, concertos, sonatas and chamber music) Prokofiev has written extensively for stage and screen, and orchestral excerpts from these works appear with some regularity on concert programs. Some of these are *Alexander Nevsky*, *Lieutenant Kije* (motion picture scores), *Love for Three Oranges* (fairy tale opera), *War and Peace* (opera after Tolstoy's gigantic novel) and *Romeo and Juliet* (very popular ballet after Shakespeare's play). After the Russian revolution, Prokofiev left Russia, first for America, and later settled in Paris. However, he returned to Moscow in 1935 and is now considered a Soviet composer.

Perhaps the most significant name in music of the first half of the twentieth century is Igor Stravinsky (1882–1971). Like the artist, Picasso, he worked effectively in a great variety of styles. His early works show the influences of Romanticism, especially the nationalistic aspect, and, to a lesser extent, of impressionism. He studied briefly with Rimsky-Korsakov for whom he had great respect and admiration, but otherwise was largely self-taught. He seemed always to be aware of everything going on in music, new and old, and was always able to adapt to his own usage anything he thought of value. "Adapt" is really an inadequate word as applied to Stravinsky, for he brought to any material a prodigious originality and transformed it completely.

The early works include the symphonic poem, *Fireworks*, and some of his important ballets— *The Firebird, Petrouchka, Le Sacre du Printemps* (*The Rite of Spring*) and *Les Noces* (*Weddings*), all based on Russian folklore. These were composed at the urging of Diaghilev, impresario (managing director) of the *Ballets Russes*. The first two were quite successful, but the third, *The Rite of Spring*, caused a riotous demonstration at its first performance. Dissonance, polytonality, wild rhythms and polyrhythms (simultaneous use of different rhythms), crude orchestral sound—all completely appropriate to the subject matter which deals with primitive, pagan fertility rites in ancient Russia—proved too much for many in that first audience. Stravinsky had used these devices before—just a hint in *Firebird*, more liberally in *Petrouchka*, but not enough to arouse such hostility. Time, however, has helped us grow accustomed to what was so shocking in 1913. And many composers have since gone much further along these lines than Stravinsky.

Next he turned away from works for large orchestra with heavily programmatic background, and worked in more abstract Classic forms for smaller instrumental (and/or vocal) combinations. The ballet *Pulcinella*, based on themes by Pergolesi and another called *Apollon Musagète*, the *Symphony of Psalms* and the opera-oratorio, *Oedipus Rex*, are in this more austere, Classic style. He made occasional use of American jazz styles, and in some of his later works he wrote "serial" music which we will discuss a little further on. Whatever the style, his skill and knowledge remain undisputed, but it is the early ballets that remain consistently popular with concert audiences. After the Russian revolution in 1917 Stravinsky never returned to his native land. He became first a French citizen and later a naturalized American.

Dmitri Shostakovich (1906–   ) was born and has lived his whole life in Russia and so is truly a Soviet composer. His two most popular works are his *First Symphony*, written when he was nineteen years old, and his *Fifth Symphony*. His work makes moderate use of dissonance and other modern techniques and is generally Classic in form. He has a gift for melody, often quite lyric, sometimes impish and caustic. His rhythms are inventive, bold, and assertive. His music is dramatic, tender, powerful and even recklessly exciting. He admires Beethoven, considering him a "people's composer" and several of his symphonies have choral endings, in the style of Beethoven's *Ninth*. Both he and Prokofiev have occasionally been criticized in official Soviet papers as being too "bourgeois" and formalistic, and Shostakovich has had to redefine publicly his artistic purposes. However, he has also been honored with great recognition by the Soviet government.

*   *   *

Expressionism developed as a reaction to impressionism. It is supposed to concern itself with the "expression" of the most subjective emotions and is therefore more directly assertive than are the vague and sometimes sentimental moods of impressionism. Expressionist music is generally boldly dissonant, rhythmically angular, often instrumentally harsh. Although it had begun to appear somewhat earlier, it derived much nourishment from the ever increasing mechanization and the terrible wars that characterized the twentieth century. The music (and other expressionist art) takes on a satirical bite or a weird and ghastly humor that is really a form of protest against "dehumanization" by war and machines.

Arnold Schoenberg (1874–1951), Austrian born, traditionally trained post-Wagnerian composer, is unquestionably among the most interesting of the composers called "expressionists" although he might have objected to the label. He developed a system of composition based on the assumption that no one of the twelve different notes found in the span of one octave should be more important than any other, thus demolishing the concept of key (as described in Chapter II—section on harmony) where the notes have relatively greater or lesser importance and one becomes the most important of all. The system is referred to as the twelve-tone or dodecaphonic system and the atonal music it produces is called serial music. Schoenberg also developed a method of writing for voices called *sprechstimme* (song-speech) where the voice part is partly spoken and partly sung in an almost random manner. While his serial works have never achieved great popularity, the dodecaphonic system and Arnold Schoenberg's teaching have had

153

tremendous influence on the work of many twentieth century composers. His early and rather traditional work, *Verklärte Nacht* (*Transfigured Night*), is performed and has won great recognition as a ballet called *Pillar of Fire.*

Alban Berg (1885–1935), a pupil of Schoenberg, is best known for his opera *Wozzeck*, a depressing tale of a soldier who is a born loser. Berg uses the serial technique, but not so strictly as his teacher. The result is somewhat more lyric, and *Wozzeck* contains many very touching passages.

Anton Webern (1883–1945) also composed serial music. Realizing that the technique required a whole new approach to form, he sought to condense things into structures so brief they often seem like mere fragments. But they are extremely interesting, with startling instrumental effects, strange but compelling harmonies (or dissonances) and very complicated rhythms.

The serial technique has attracted many other composers. Most of them have used it as another device or idiom capable of producing special effects, but not as a system dominating an entire composition. It is in this role that it is likely to have its greatest influence since compositions that are entirely serial tend to sound similar and often monotonous.

*　　*　　*

Another twentieth century idiom is American jazz, and this leads us to a brief consideration of American music in general. Books have been written on the history of American music. Our concern, however, is listening, so we will touch on only a few pertinent aspects. During the seventeenth century the colonists were busy building and surviving, and music centered mainly around the church and the remembered songs of the mother country. When you consider that the mother countries included England, Holland, Spain and France, the cultural mix was a rich one. Add to it the native influence of the American Indian and the imported African influence of the slaves, and the results were bound to be unique. However, they took time to develop and meanwhile the colonies, and after the Revolution, the states, imported their music from Europe. Thomas Jefferson was a talented amateur musician who arranged and played in chamber music concerts at his home, and Lorenzo da Ponte, librettist for some of Mozart's operas, taught Italian at Columbia University in New York in the early nineteenth century. For the most part, our composers studied abroad and their styles were much influenced by their European teachers. It was in the area of less formal music that recognizable American styles began to emerge. Minstrel songs, plantation songs, spirituals, cowboy songs, country music are all the products of a mixture of a local or regional culture and one or more of the ethnic or national backgrounds previously mentioned. Much of such music was truly folk, having developed from the efforts of untrained and unknown amateurs. But some composers were able to catch the color and spirit of the folk music. Foremost among these was Stephen Foster (1826–1864) whose songs evoke a vivid picture of the pre-Civil War era in American history.

Precisely because of the hugeness of this country, where whole sections developed separately and under different cultural influences, the United States, still young as great nations go, has not yet developed a national musical style. Coming of age musically in the twentieth century, it is doubtful that it ever will. For the twentieth century, as we have already said, has been and continues to be a period of musical experimentation, especially in the realm of serious music, and experimentation has a highly individual character rather than a national one.

Nevertheless, one aspect of this country's music has been universally labeled "American" and that is jazz. Again, jazz has been the subject of many books and we cannot detail its long history here. It derived from strong African influences, by way of minstrel songs, ragtime and blues. An insistent beat with syncopated rhythms, melodies enriched with improvised embellishments, instrumentation that features the saxophone, trumpet, trombone, piano, banjo, guitar and drums, and harmonies that pepper major keys with chords that belong in minor keys—these are the marks of jazz. Through the years there have appeared different styles of this popular music, sometimes more improvisational (Dixieland, and later, swing), sometimes more strictly written out (big band era of sophisticated arrangements), sometimes more heavily rhythmic (by means of electric amplification) and more simplistic harmonically (rock)—but the basic ingredients remain the same and the stamp remains "American." Besides making its international mark in its own right, jazz has attracted the interest of many serious composers of many nationalities. Milhaud, Ravel and Stravinsky are among those who have used jazz styles in important works. George Gershwin (1898–1937), noted composer of popular Broadway musical shows, lifted jazz to symphonic proportions with such works as *Rhapsody in Blue, American in Paris* and *Concerto in F*.

Edward MacDowell (1861–1908) was most notable among the nineteenth century American composers under strong European influence. In some short works like the *Woodland Sketches* for piano he includes an occasional piece such as *From an Indian Lodge*, but his *Second Piano Concerto* is firmly in the tradition of German Romanticism.

The most startlingly original American is Charles Ives (1874–1954), an insurance broker and prolific spare time composer who experimented with atonality, polytonality, polyrhythms and most of the twentieth century techniques long before his European counterparts "discovered" them.

Since contemporary music has taken on a kind of international similarity due to its preoccupation with experimental techniques and systems, many American composers have now achieved worldwide recognition. Leonard Bernstein, Samuel Barber, Gian-Carlo Menotti, Roy Harris, Aaron Copland, Elliott Carter, Henry Cowell are just a few of these.

* * *

The attempt to break away from old forms has resulted in some radical changes. So far we have considered only new ways of handling the traditional elements described in Chapter II—melody, rhythm, harmony, tone color and dynamics—as applied to traditional musical instruments and the voice. But the twentieth century is exploring wholly new avenues. Some composers are writing aleatoric music. Aleatoric means "by chance" and indicates that the composer wants the performer to play anything he chooses for a given section of the music. The concept is not entirely new, since the cadenza of the Classic concerto (Chapter XI) permitted the performer to improvise. However he was expected to use the themes of the concerto and to respect the style of the composer. Also, a good deal of improvisation takes place in jazz, but, here too, the players are expected to stay within the harmonic and melodic boundaries of the piece. In aleatoric music there are no restrictions whatever, nor is its application limited to a soloist's cadenza. Imagine, therefore, a hundred piece symphony orchestra playing on an "every man for himself" basis and you can begin to see some of the possibilities.

The twentieth century composer, more tolerant of dissonance than his immediate ancestors, now feels that the whole world of sound is the legitimate material of music. An ambulance siren, the roar of an engine, the factory sounds of heavy industry, crowd noises— anything audible can be caught on tape recorders, amplified to any dynamic level, changed to any pitch level and distorted to any desired tone quality by altering the tape speed and manipulating the amplification. These new sounds can then be used either in combination with traditional instruments or entirely in combination with each other to produce a new electronic music. Sound can also be produced originally by electronic means. The Hammond organ, for instance, produces sound without pipes or reeds, but purely electronically. When modern computer techniques are added to electronic sound generators in instruments called synthesizers, the possibilities for new sounds are literally limitless. And, one may also say without being facetious, so are the possibilities for silence and monotony. Many of the new so called *avant garde* works have long stretches of silence or of a single note varied only in dynamics or tone color.

Much of the musical *avant garde* makes its appeal more directly to the senses than to the intellect and so links up rather readily with the *avant garde* in the various other arts. We get what are referred to as happenings which combine dance, theatre arts, visual arts including projections, light-play, painting, sculpture— all these highly abstract— and often the most random and aleatoric audience participation.

Traditionalists question whether much of the *avant garde* is music at all, since they find it bizarre and grotesque and lacking in everything they feel is beautiful. But it is unusual, very often interesting, evoking moods and reactions quite unlike the music we have previously considered.

Some of the composers who work in this field are John Cage, Karlheinz Stockhausen, Milton Babbit, Pierre Boulez, Edgar Varèse, Vladimir Ussachevsky, Luciano Berio and Otto Luening.

* * *

We have mentioned some of the *avant garde* composers, some American composers and some of the most important of the internationally recognized twentieth century "giants." Other names should be included in this last category, because their works appear with some regularity on concert programs. Béla Bartók (1881–1945) was a Hungarian who mixed almost all the modern techniques with Hungarian folk music ideas. Best known among his works are the *Concerto for Orchestra* and *Music for Strings, Percussion and Celesta*. Paul Hindemith (1895–1963) was a German, basically a neo-Classicist, who composed much chamber music and many important orchestral works including a great symphony called *Mathis der Maler*. Benjamin Britten (1913–   ) is the English composer of *Young Person's Guide to the Orchestra*, but his reputation rests chiefly on his operas, *Death in Venice, Peter Grimes* and *Albert Herring* among them. Alberto Ginastera (1916–   ) is an Argentine also known for his operas. Heitor Villa-Lobos (1871–1959) was a Brazilian who combined native Brazilian folk styles (Negro, Indian and Portugese) with sophisticated modern but not radical techniques, often with very exciting and beautiful effect as in the *Bachianas Brasileiras #5* for soprano and eight cellos, where he flavors Brazilian material with elements of Bach's style.

These composers added to those already mentioned comprise a very meagre list of the multitude who have produced or are producing modern serious music. It is difficult from our very close perspective amid the confusion created by so many experiments to predict whose work will be lasting and timeless and which, if any, of the new techniques and idioms will prove permanently significant. We should, however, remember that Berlioz and Wagner were considered pretty "far out" by many of their contemporaries and at least try to listen with open mind and ears.

XV

HOW HI THE FI?

Sooner or later most listeners begin to collect their own records or tapes and so we are including a chapter on sound reproducing equipment. The quality of such equipment is generally judged by the fidelity with which it reproduces the sound produced by the live performer. But the words high-fidelity or hi-fi have been used so loosely in commercial advertising that they no longer have much meaning. The purchaser of such equipment, therefore, must be prepared to judge it for himself.

It is something like buying a car. Do you want the basic minimum auto that will provide the most economical transportation? Do you consider comfort more important? Perhaps high style is your thing, and you choose a car for its color, lines and trim. Or maybe it's power and speed you're after. The fact remains that cars are marketed to suit a wide variety of needs and tastes over a wide range of prices. This is true, too, of sound equipment. Let us look at some of the factors involved and terms you should be familiar with when you are ready to buy.

Recording began about 1880 with an accoustical process wherein a needle activated by sound vibrations made cuts on a cylinder or disc which could then be played back. These early records are now collectors' items but they sound terrible by present day standards. (They are kinder to the human voice than to instruments.) It wasn't until 1924 that the use of microphones and electrical equipment rendered possible any degree of realistic orchestral sound. Since then a never ending series of technical improvements has brought us the long playing record, electro-magnetic tape recording, and an ever increasing faithfulness in the reproduction of actual concert hall sound.

However, styles and tastes change. With the advent of the sound movie (and, more especially, of the movie musical), audiences became accustomed to the amplified, "surrounding" sound of the movie theatre. In the larger houses extra speakers were frequently used to insure good audibility throughout the auditorium and to avoid echoes, and so the music came at you from all sides. As audiences became used to the stereophonic effect, it was introduced into the recording of serious music through the use of two speakers placed some distance apart. The knowledge that the sounds produced by an orchestra spread out on a large stage come at you from different directions provided an added justification. This directional effect, however, is minimal in the concert hall. Most conductors strive hard to achieve a blended, balanced and focused sound. When a composer calls for a special directional or antiphonal effect, the conductor groups his musicians accordingly, perhaps placing some offstage or at the back of the auditorium or in a balcony. Thus, while it is possible in stereo recording for an engineer to separate the orchestral sounds in tracks so that the oboe and violins come to you through the left speaker and the cellos and horn through the right, this is an exaggeration of the very slight directional effect of the concert hall. The older monaural recordings (one track—one speaker) actually came closer to the composer's and conductor's intentions for a focused sound. However, since the demand for stereo is great, monaural equipment and recordings are being phased out, and one is forced to buy stereo. The taste for the lush "surrounding" sound continues unabated, reinforced, perhaps, by the vogue of heavy amplification in the rock styles, and so "quadraphonic" recordings calling for four speakers have been placed on the market.

Fidelity can be measured in highly technical terms dealing with cycles, frequencies, wattage output, decibel levels, etc. These are objective scientific measurements of the responsiveness of the equipment to the range, volume and tone quality of the sounds being reproduced. Cheap equipment might not respond to very high or very low pitches (frequencies) and might distort the sound at very high or very low volume. The equipment is frequently sold as separate components so that one must buy an amplifier, sometimes a pre-amplifier, an A.M., F.M. tuner (if one wants to include radio), a record player consisting of a turntable, tone arm and a needle cartridge, a tape deck (if one wants to play tapes or be able to record), and speakers. Each of these components, then, is part of a chain. If any link in the chain is inadequate in any way, the quality of the entire chain is reduced. If, for example, the needle is dull, the best speakers and amplifiers will only be able to project the sound of a dull needle. If the amplifier is of poor quality, the other components are brought down to that level. If the speakers are "out of phase" the sound is not quite right. And since equipment of this sort is both delicate and complicated, the enthusiast who goes in for expensive components should have sufficient technical "know how" to be able to pinpoint difficulties if they arise and make the necessary repairs and adjustments.

Most of us are not so gifted. Fortunately, many manufacturers of audio equipment recognize this and assemble complete and self-contained units of good quality that are less delicate and complicated than separate components.

The question then is, "What to buy?" This becomes a very individual matter and might well begin with how much you are willing or can afford to spend. Next you should determine what services you require. In some parts of our country radio carries very little serious music, and you might want only a record player. In other areas, there is much good music on radio but mostly on F.M. (or mostly on A.M. as the case may be). Here you'd want to include a good radio, A.M. or F.M. as needed or both, and possibly a tape deck so you could record music from broadcasts. Or perhaps you prefer tape to disc recording and can therefore dispense with a turntable altogether. Tapes (cartridges and casettes) store more easily than discs but they're more expensive and the catalogue of available titles is not as extensive as for disc records.

As for quality, one should consult any reputable consumer's guide such as *Consumer Reports* or those more specifically given to rating audio equipment. But, a word of warning: these ratings are based on the scientific and technical measurements mentioned earlier, not all of which are easily audible even to the most trained ear. You may be paying for a degree of fidelity greater than you can hear or appreciate. So, in the final analysis, you should listen to several different sets of equipment, make comparisons and select what suits you best. If you have reached this point in the book, and have listened to a number of the works described to which you diligently applied some of the listening techniques outlined, you have already developed some valid critical standards and you can trust them.

Finally, a word about recordings, tape or disc. You buy a record for repeated playings, so buy those works for which you have a great affection or which challenge you in some way to get to know them better. Buy good quality records, because even the finest equipment can't make a poor recording sound much better than it is. Remember that the latest isn't always the best. The same work may be recorded by a dozen different orchestras or artists. An older recording may be a finer interpretation or have a better over-all sound than the latest one, and often it is less expensive.

Listen to your records with your friends. Trying to convey your enthusiasms to others frequently gives you new and deeper insights, and exchanging comments can build new awareness.

While not every participant listener must be a record collector, there are few collectors of records of serious music who are not participant listeners.

XVI

MUSIC AND TRAVEL

We started this book with a visit to a concert at Tanglewood in Massachusetts, and since travel is so much a part of today's lifestyles it seems fitting that we should close with a word about music and travel, especially vacation travel.

In many parts of Europe, places of historic and/or musical significance are the scene of long established summer music festivals. In America and some of the younger countries the historic appeal is less important, but places of great natural beauty with attractive summer climates also feature elaborate music programs. Many of these programs are built around famous orchestras or great virtuosi, but many also include or are built around highly professional and distinguished summer music schools and feature young and exciting new talent. Taking in an occasional concert, opera or ballet performance while on a trip can enrich the trip immeasurably and provide a great deal of musical pleasure as well. One gets to see and mingle with the local citizenry as well as with tourists under circumstances quite different from daytime sight-seeing or museum and cathedral hopping, and the rewards are almost always greater than the local movie, theater or night club would yield.

The many festivals vary so much in size and importance that we can touch only on the best known.

Tanglewood in Lenox, Massachusetts, is the home of the Berkshire Festival and is built around the Boston Symphony Orchestra, but also features a first rate summer music school from which have emerged many important artists.

Saratoga Performing Arts Center in Saratoga Springs, New York offers the New York City Ballet and the Philadelphia Symphony

Orchestra. This great orchestra also performs *al fresco* (in the open air) in Robin Hood Dell in Philadelphia.

A varied program of chamber music, soloists, orchestra and opera (often unusual ones) is presented in the lovely garden of the Rosen estate at Caramoor in Katonah, N.Y. Here a beautiful Renaissance stage has been constructed and performances on summer weekends are not only excellent, but have an air of old-world elegance about them.

New York City is the home of the Metropolitan Opera and the New York Philharmonic Orchestra, and both organizations have appeared in early summer programs in their home auditoriums in Lincoln Center as well as in free performances in the city parks where one can also enjoy free Shakespeare performances, a jazz festival and the Goldman Band.

The Kennedy Center in Washington D.C. affords the tourist who is visiting the nation's capital a chance to hear the National Symphony Orchestra as well as many other groups.

Marlboro, Vermont presents chamber music by some of the world's greatest artists in truly rustic surroundings.

The Chicago Symphony Orchestra appears in Ravinia Park in Chicago and the Los Angeles Philharmonic gives concerts at the Hollywood Bowl in Los Angeles.

The National Music Camp at Interlocken, Michigan is a summer music school for talented youngsters from all over the country. Their oldest and most advanced groups appear in concert and are astonishingly good.

Among the more spectacular settings for great musical performance in this country is Aspen, Colorado, deep in the Rocky Mountains, where a fine summer school and appearances by important artists are featured; in Santa Fe, New Mexico, opera is performed in a breath-taking setting.

In Europe you have only to pick your location, the city or country you most want to visit, and you will almost certainly find something of combined historical and musical interest very nearby.

If one has a taste for opera and the spectacular, one should not miss a performance of *Aida* in the Baths of Caracalla in Rome. Here the massive Egyptian setting is made to blend in with the fortress-like walls of the ruined Baths so that, while the action is confined to the stage, the background is vast and ancient and far more realistic than in any opera house. The acoustics are not perfect (they use amplification), the performance not always the best, but the over-all effect is unbeatable. They also perform other operas here. In Verona, performances of opera are given in a huge old Roman amphitheatre in a fine state of preservation. For those who like opera on a more intimate scale Glyndebourne, England offers performances in a formal English garden setting that have earned a reputation for being the ultimate in authentic style and taste. And, of course, Wagnerites flock to Bayreuth, Germany for performances of the master's music dramas in the amazingly suitable *Festspielhaus* (Festival Playhouse) designed by Wagner himself and built especially for him by King Ludwig of Bavaria.

More varied musical fare is available at the world famous Salzburg Festival. This lovely old Austrian city was Mozart's birthplace and is the home of a great music school, the *Mozarteum*. The festival features the world's greatest artists and conductors in operatic, symphonic, chamber music and solo performances and does not limit itself to Mozart's music.

Similar festivals are held in many European cities. Most notable are those of Edinburgh in Scotland, Spoleto and Florence in Italy, Bergen (Grieg's birthplace) in Norway and Dubrovnick in Yugoslavia. Performances are given in the great halls of old castles, in palace gardens or courtyards, and in historic old theatres or churches. Here and there one finds performances in exciting modern auditoriums as well as remodeled and rebuilt old ones. Some of the more interesting and beautiful auditoriums are worth a special visit, with or without a performance. The elaborate and handsome Paris Opera, the elegantly rebuilt Vienna State Opera house (severely damaged in World War II), the smaller but gemlike *La Fenice* in Venice, the stately *La Scala* in Milan and the modern Festival Hall in London, are examples. If one gets as far south as Australia, Sydney's music center with its controversial opera house is of great architectural as well as musical interest.

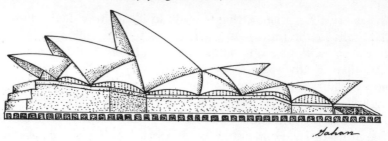

*Opera at sea. The Opera House at Sydney, Australia where the building
shape was inspired via billowing sails.*

Nearer home is South America where our summer is their winter
and thus the height of their musical season. Buenos Aires, Rio de
Janeiro and all the great capitals not only boast fine resident musical
organizations, but they are also regular stops on the international
circuit of all the great artists.

Some travel agencies arrange special music tours which take in
the important festivals or other musical events and which include
not only the usual sight-seeing, but admission to the major musical
offerings.

So, if you travel, music can be an important and enjoyable part
of your trip. Bon Voyage!

*   *   *

THE PARTICIPANT LISTENER'S
LIST AND INDEX OF
COMPOSERS AND COMPOSITIONS

Following is a list of works which can serve as the basis for a record collection. Specific recordings are not suggested since you may want to exercise your own taste and judgment, particularly if you have developed preferences for particular conductors, orchestras or soloists. Besides, new recordings of many of these works are constantly being released. Where operas and ballets are listed, the listener is reminded that recordings of excerpts, highlights, or suites are available.

The list consists of all the compositions mentioned in the text. Those titles marked with an asterisk we consider most basic. If you are beginning a collection, these might be the recordings you would want to acquire first. The listing is by composer, in alphabetical order, with year of birth in parentheses and page reference following. The page of chief reference for each composer is underlined.

*   *   *

The following is a list of composers mentioned in the text for whom no specific compositions are cited. This is not because they produced no works of interest or importance, but simply because there was room only for the limited number of examples used. Indeed, the field is so vast that this and the preceding list together still leave many gaps.

GENERAL INDEX

General Index

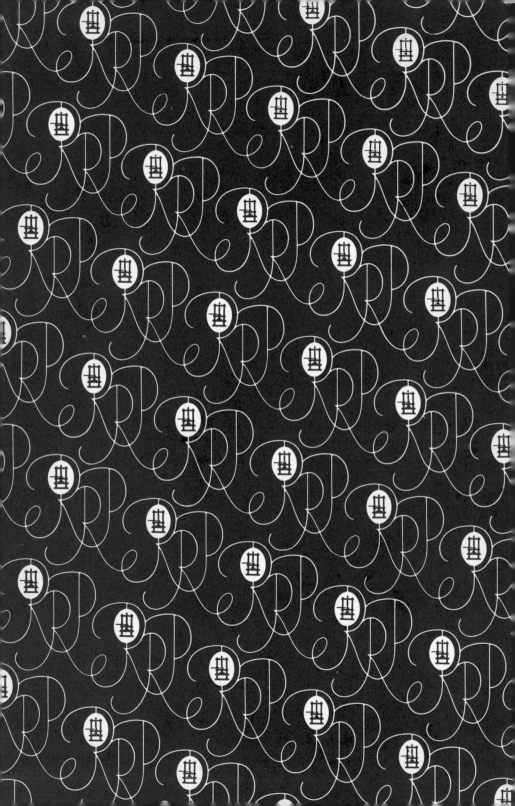